Navigating the World of Offline and Online Shopping

C. P. Kumar
Reiki Healer
Roorkee - 247667, India

Disclaimer

While every effort has been made to ensure the accuracy and completeness of the content in this book, the author cannot guarantee that the information contained herein is error-free, up-to-date, or suitable for every individual circumstance.

The author shall not be held liable or responsible for any errors or omissions in the content of the book, nor for any damages, or losses that may arise from any actions taken based upon the suggestions or contents presented in the book.

Readers are advised to use their own judgment and discretion in applying the information provided in this book, and to consult with qualified professionals before taking any action based on the contents of this book. The author disclaims any and all liability or responsibility for any actions taken or not taken based on the information contained in this book.

DEDICATION

To all those who embark on the fascinating journey of shopping, whether in the bustling aisles of brick-and-mortar stores or the virtual realms of online marketplaces, this book is dedicated to you.

In the ever-evolving landscape of commerce, where traditions and technologies intertwine, your curiosity and discerning choices shape the retail world. Your preferences, desires, and expectations drive innovation and transformation, impacting not only the way you shop but the very essence of shopping itself.

As we delve into the intricate realm of "Navigating the World of Offline and Online Shopping", it is your inquisitiveness and eagerness to explore these dynamic domains that have inspired this journey. With this book, we aim to provide a comprehensive understanding of the multifaceted universe of shopping, from its historical roots to the exciting possibilities that lie ahead.

Your curiosity fuels our exploration of consumer psychology, technological trends, innovative retail experiences, and the ethical considerations that define the shopping experience. Your demand for convenience and safety pushes us to examine payment methods, security, and customer service in both the online and offline spheres. Your commitment to sustainability and ethical choices drives our discussions on responsible consumerism and its impact on the environment and society.

In an age where shopping is as much a personal expression as a practical necessity, we acknowledge your significance as the ultimate decision-makers, and we are dedicated to helping you make informed, empowered choices. May the insights within these pages guide you through the ever-shifting terrain of retail, equipping you with the knowledge and confidence to navigate the shopping world with wisdom and discernment.

Your quest for the perfect purchase and your contribution to the shaping of the future of shopping are celebrated within these chapters. To you, the intrepid shopper, we dedicate this book.

With heartfelt gratitude and appreciation,

C. P. Kumar

CONTENTS

PREFACE

In a world constantly in flux, where traditional and digital domains converge, shopping is an ever-evolving landscape. This book, "Navigating the World of Offline and Online Shopping", is your passport to explore this transformative journey, one that begins in the familiar aisles of brick-and-mortar stores and extends to the boundless aisles of the internet. This book's purpose is to be your guiding light on this expedition, helping you comprehend the vast ocean of opportunities, challenges, and choices that await you in the realm of shopping.

The purpose of this book is to serve as your trusty companion as you embark on a comprehensive exploration of the shopping universe. It equips you with the knowledge and insights to make informed decisions, providing a well-rounded understanding of the multifaceted shopping landscape. Whether you're a seasoned shopper or someone just setting out on their retail journey, this book offers a treasure trove of information and strategies to navigate both the offline and online worlds.

The significance of this book lies in its ability to provide a holistic perspective on shopping. It encompasses the historical evolution of shopping, consumer psychology, and the current trends in both offline and online shopping. It offers insights into the advantages and disadvantages of physical stores, as well as the innovation occurring in response to online competition. This book further explores the integration of offline and online shopping experiences, and the role of mobile devices, e-commerce platforms, and payment methods in shaping the modern shopping landscape.

The book also delves into crucial aspects of trust, security, and privacy in online shopping, as well as the influence of social media, customer reviews, and price comparison on shopping decisions. It also addresses issues related to returns, customer service, fraud prevention, ethical shopping, and sustainability. Ultimately, it speculates on the future of shopping, offering a glimpse into how emerging technologies and changing consumer expectations might transform the retail landscape.

The significance of this book lies in its ability to empower you with knowledge, strategies, and a comprehensive understanding of the evolving world of shopping. It provides a roadmap for making informed choices, saving money, and ensuring your shopping experiences are safe and ethical. Whether you're a savvy shopper looking to enhance your skills or someone taking their first steps into the world of commerce, this book offers valuable insights and guidance. It's not just a book; it's a tool for navigating the dynamic and ever-changing world of shopping.

C. P. Kumar
Reiki Healer
Former Scientist 'G', National Institute of Hydrology
Roorkee - 247667, India
Web: https://www.angelfire.com/nh/cpkumar/virgo.html

Chapter 1. Introduction to Shopping Trends

In a world constantly propelled by technological innovations, shopping has undergone a profound transformation, evolving from traditional brick-and-mortar stores to the limitless expanse of online marketplaces. The journey of shopping trends is a reflection of the changing dynamics in consumer behavior, the influence of e-commerce giants, and the growing importance of convenience in the modern era. As we embark on this exploration of shopping trends, we will traverse the historical context of shopping, highlighting the shifts from physical stores to digital platforms and discussing the factors driving these changes.

The Historical Context of Shopping Trends

To understand the shopping trends of today, it is crucial to delve into the historical roots of consumer behavior. For centuries, shopping took place in local markets and small stores, offering a limited selection of goods, primarily catering to the needs of a local community. However, this all changed with the advent of the industrial revolution in the 18th and 19th centuries.

1. The Birth of Retail: From Local Markets to Department Stores

The industrial revolution brought forth an array of technological advancements, such as the steam engine and the assembly line (manufacturing process in which a product is progressively built by moving it through a series of workstations, with each station performing a specific task), which led to mass production and a burgeoning middle class with increased purchasing power. As a result, the concept of shopping expanded beyond local markets. The first notable shift was the emergence of department stores, such as Macy's (American department store chain) and Harrods (luxury department store in the United Kingdom), which introduced the idea of centralized shopping with a wide range of products under one roof. These stores became destinations for socializing, offering not only products but also an experience.

2. Mail-Order Catalogs and the Birth of E-commerce

Mail-order catalogs are printed publications that list and describe products for sale, allowing customers to order items by mail for delivery to their homes. While department stores thrived in urban areas, mail-order catalogs like Sears and Roebuck (a prominent American retail company that operated department stores and mail-order catalogs, particularly in the 20th century) brought the convenience of shopping to rural areas. Consumers could peruse catalogs and place orders via mail. This marked an early precursor to e-commerce as it eliminated the need to visit physical stores. However, this method was limited in its scope and had its own set of challenges.

The Evolution of Shopping: From E-commerce to Online Marketplaces

The true revolution in shopping trends came with the advent of the internet and the proliferation of online retail platforms. This transformation has been driven by various factors, each contributing to the shift from traditional brick-and-mortar stores to online marketplaces.

1. Convenience: The Primary Driver of Online Shopping

Perhaps the most significant factor influencing the shift to online shopping has been the unparalleled convenience it offers. Online shoppers can browse, compare, and purchase products from the comfort of their own homes, at any time, day or night. With just a few clicks, they can have items delivered to their doorsteps, eliminating the need for time-consuming trips to physical stores.

2. Expansive Product Selection

Online marketplaces have virtually infinite shelf space compared to physical stores. The vast assortment of products available online, from around the world, allows consumers to find precisely what they need and discover new items they might not encounter in their local stores.

3. Price Comparison and Competitive Shopping

The ability to easily compare prices across different online retailers empowers consumers to make more informed purchasing decisions. This feature has prompted intense competition among e-commerce platforms, further benefiting consumers through lower prices and exclusive deals.

4. Personalization and Data-Driven Shopping

E-commerce platforms are online software solutions that enable businesses to set up, manage, and run their digital stores, facilitating online buying and selling of products or services. e-commerce platforms employ sophisticated algorithms to track consumer behavior and preferences, enabling personalized product recommendations. This level of personalization enhances the shopping experience, making it easier for consumers to find products that align with their tastes and needs.

5. The Rise of Online Marketplaces and Third-Party Sellers

The advent of online marketplaces, led by giants like Amazon and eBay, has revolutionized how consumers interact with online shopping. These platforms serve as intermediaries, connecting buyers and sellers from around the world. This model has expanded e-commerce even further, fostering the growth of independent sellers and small businesses.

The Blurred Lines Between Offline and Online Shopping

The dichotomy between offline and online shopping is not as clear-cut as it once was. With the advancement of technology, both realms have started to converge, leading to an omnichannel shopping experience. *Omnichannel shopping* refers to a retail strategy that integrates multiple sales and marketing channels to provide a seamless and consistent shopping experience for customers, whether they shop in physical stores, online, through mobile apps, or other channels. The following factors illustrate the blurring lines between traditional and online shopping.

1. Brick-and-Click Retailers

Many traditional brick-and-mortar stores have embraced online sales, creating an integrated shopping experience. Consumers can shop online and pick up their purchases in-store or return online purchases at physical locations. This hybrid approach caters to the diverse preferences of modern consumers.

2. Augmented Reality and Virtual Reality

Technological innovations like augmented reality (AR) and virtual reality (VR) have made it possible for consumers to visualize products and try them out virtually. *Augmented Reality* (AR) enhances the real world by overlaying digital information, images, or objects onto a user's view through devices like smartphones or AR glasses. *Virtual Reality* (VR) immerses users in a computer-generated, simulated environment, isolating them from the physical world, often through headsets or goggles. These technologies enhance the online shopping experience by bridging the gap between seeing a product in-store and experiencing it online.

3. Social Commerce

Social media platforms have become a significant player in the world of online shopping. Many businesses now use platforms like Instagram and Facebook to showcase products and even enable in-app purchases. Consumers can discover and purchase products directly from their social media feeds.

The Future of Shopping Trends

As we look to the future, shopping trends are likely to continue evolving. The integration of emerging technologies and the evolving expectations of consumers will shape the landscape of both offline and online shopping.

1. Sustainability and Ethical Shopping

Consumers are increasingly conscious of the environmental and ethical implications of their purchases. Brands and retailers that embrace sustainable and ethical practices will likely gain favor with consumers, and the shopping landscape may see a shift towards more responsible consumption.

2. Voice Commerce and Artificial Intelligence

Voice-activated smart devices, such as Amazon's Alexa and Apple's Siri, are making it easier for consumers to shop through voice commands. With the integration of artificial intelligence, these devices can understand and fulfill shopping requests, simplifying the shopping process further.

3. Drones and Autonomous Delivery

The use of drones and autonomous vehicles for delivery is gaining momentum. This innovation has the potential to expedite the delivery process, making it even more convenient for consumers. Amazon, for example, has been testing drone delivery services in select areas.

4. The Influence of Social Media and Influencer Marketing

Social media platforms continue to impact shopping trends. Influencer marketing, where individuals with large followings promote products, is a powerful tool for reaching and engaging consumers. Brands are expected to increasingly utilize these platforms for marketing and sales.

5. Enhanced Data Security and Privacy Concerns

As online shopping continues to expand, data security and privacy concerns become more critical. Consumers will expect a high level of security for their personal information and financial transactions. Businesses that prioritize data security will likely gain trust and loyalty from consumers.

Conclusion: Navigating the World of Shopping Trends

Shopping has come a long way from the days of local markets and department stores. The evolution of shopping trends, from the rise of e-commerce to the convergence of online and offline shopping, showcases the dynamic nature of consumer behavior and the influence of technology.

As we navigate the world of offline and online shopping, it's clear that the lines between the two are increasingly blurry. Consumers today enjoy the convenience and variety of online shopping, while still cherishing the experience of physical stores. The future of shopping will undoubtedly be marked by further technological advancements, a focus on sustainability and ethics, and the ever-growing influence of social media.

In this dynamic landscape, businesses must adapt and innovate to meet the changing expectations of consumers. Shopping trends will continue to evolve, and those who stay ahead of the curve will be best positioned to thrive in the world of retail.

Introduction

Shopping is an intrinsic part of human existence, driven not only by necessity but by an array of complex psychological factors. Whether it's a stroll through a bustling mall or the click of a mouse in the comfort of one's own home, the act of shopping is more than just a transactional experience. It's a multifaceted process that encompasses an array of emotions, motivations, and decision-making mechanisms. This article will delve into the psychology of shopping, exploring consumer behavior and decision-making processes in both offline and online shopping environments. By understanding the intricate workings of the consumer mind, we can gain valuable insights into how to navigate the world of offline and online shopping successfully.

The Intrinsic Connection between Emotions and Shopping

Emotions play a significant role in shaping shopping behavior, both offline and online. When consumers enter a store or browse an e-commerce website, their emotional states influence their decisions. Here's a closer look at the emotional aspects of shopping:

1. Retail Therapy: The Emotional Escape

Retail therapy is a well-known phenomenon wherein individuals shop to alleviate stress, boost their mood, or escape from daily life pressures. Offline shopping provides immediate gratification through sensory experiences, like touching fabrics or smelling perfumes. Online shopping offers convenience, allowing consumers to indulge in retail therapy from the comfort of their own homes.

2. FOMO and Social Influence

Fear of Missing Out (FOMO) is a potent emotion that drives people to make impulse purchases. Social media platforms and online shopping often exacerbate FOMO, as consumers witness their peers' purchases and experiences, compelling them to partake. In physical stores, peer pressure and the desire to conform to fashion trends can trigger spontaneous buying.

The Decision-Making Process in Offline Shopping

Offline shopping is a sensory-rich experience that engages multiple cognitive processes, from product selection to payment. Understanding these processes is crucial for retailers and consumers alike.

1. Store Layout and Navigation

Store layout is meticulously designed to guide consumers through a specific path. Product placement, signage, and lighting influence attention and engagement. Decision-making begins with the first step into the store, as consumers subconsciously decide which path to take.

2. The Role of Sales Associates

In physical stores, interactions with sales associates can significantly impact decision-making. Salespeople can provide recommendations, answer questions, and influence the consumer's confidence in a purchase. Personalized customer service enhances the overall shopping experience.

3. Touch and Feel

Offline shopping allows consumers to physically touch, try on, or test products. Sensory input, such as the feel of a fabric or the scent of a perfume, influences the decision-making process. The haptic experience often leads to more informed decisions and higher satisfaction.

4. Impulse Buying at Checkout

Impulse buying is common at the checkout counter, where small, low-cost items tempt consumers. This phenomenon is leveraged by retailers to increase average transaction values. Checkout area product displays are strategically designed to capitalize on this behavior.

The Decision-Making Process in Online Shopping

Online shopping has revolutionized the retail landscape, offering unparalleled convenience and a unique set of decision-making processes. Here are some key insights into online consumer behavior:

1. The Paradox of Choice

Online shopping offers an overwhelming number of choices, which can lead to choice paralysis. Consumers may spend extensive time comparing options, leading to indecision or abandonment. e-commerce platforms employ various techniques, such as filtering and sorting options, to help consumers navigate the plethora of choices.

2. The Role of Product Reviews and Social Proof

Online shoppers heavily rely on product reviews and ratings to inform their decisions. The opinions and experiences of other consumers provide social proof, influencing trust and purchase confidence. Brands and retailers need to actively manage and promote positive reviews to build trust.

3. The Influence of Algorithms and Personalization

Online retailers use recommendation algorithms to suggest products based on a user's browsing and purchase history. Personalization increases the likelihood of conversion by presenting tailored offerings. Consumers are often unaware of how these algorithms work, but they appreciate the convenience they provide.

4. Abandonment and Cart Recovery

Online shopping carts often contain items that consumers don't purchase immediately. Retailers employ strategies like cart abandonment emails to re-engage consumers and nudge them towards completing the purchase. Cart recovery tactics leverage the principles of loss aversion, reminding shoppers of the potential "loss" of their selected items.

Consumer Trust and Online Security

Trust is a fundamental component of both offline and online shopping. However, online shopping introduces unique challenges related to security and privacy.

1. Cybersecurity Concerns

Online shoppers often worry about data breaches, identity theft, and payment security. Retailers must invest in robust cybersecurity measures to safeguard consumer information.

Trust seals and secure payment options reassure consumers about the safety of their transactions.

2. The Role of User Reviews and Ratings

Authentic and transparent user reviews can build trust online. Retailers need to ensure that these reviews are unbiased and not manipulated to maintain consumer trust. A single negative review can significantly impact a potential buyer's decision.

Brand Loyalty and Post-Purchase Satisfaction

Building brand loyalty and ensuring post-purchase satisfaction are critical in both offline and online shopping environments.

1. Brand Loyalty and Offline Shopping

In physical stores, customer loyalty often arises from a combination of product quality and in-person service. Shoppers who feel valued and appreciated are more likely to return. Loyalty programs and rewards can foster brand allegiance.

2. Brand Loyalty and Online Shopping

E-commerce businesses rely on a mix of product quality, customer service, and user experience to build brand loyalty. Subscription services and exclusive offers encourage repeat purchases. The absence of in-person interaction makes consistent branding and reliable service even more critical in online shopping.

3. Post-Purchase Satisfaction and Reviews

The post-purchase experience influences a consumer's decision to return and leave reviews. An exceptional post-purchase experience can result in positive reviews, referrals, and repeat business. Addressing issues promptly and professionally can turn a negative experience into a positive one.

The Blurring Lines: Hybrid Shopping Experiences

The evolution of retail is marked by the blurring of lines between offline and online shopping. Consumers increasingly seek integrated experiences that combine the best of both worlds.

1. Omnichannel Retail

Retailers are embracing omnichannel strategies that seamlessly blend offline and online shopping. Consumers can browse online and buy in-store or vice versa, creating a holistic shopping experience. Unified inventory systems and flexible delivery options support this convergence.

2. Showrooming and Webrooming

Showrooming involves examining products in physical stores and then purchasing online. Webrooming is the opposite, where consumers research online and make in-store purchases. Both behaviors highlight the importance of aligning offline and online shopping channels.

Conclusion

The psychology of shopping is a multifaceted journey that taps into emotions, sensory experiences, and intricate decision-making processes. Whether consumers opt for offline or online shopping, understanding these intricacies is paramount for retailers and shoppers alike. From the emotional aspects that drive retail therapy to the decision-making mechanisms that shape purchases, consumers' choices are guided by a myriad of factors. As the worlds of offline and online shopping continue to evolve and interconnect, the key to success lies in adapting to changing consumer behaviors and preferences, fostering trust, and delivering exceptional post-purchase experiences. By navigating this complex landscape, retailers and consumers can unlock the true potential of the shopping experience, creating a win-win for all parties involved.

Introduction

The landscape of online shopping is rapidly changing, shaped by technological advancements and evolving consumer preferences. As we dive into the world of online retail, it's essential to understand the current and emerging trends that are revolutionizing how we shop. In this article, we will explore the dynamic online shopping trends, including the latest technological innovations and shifts in consumer behavior.

Mobile Commerce (M-Commerce)

Mobile commerce, commonly known as M-Commerce, has gained immense traction in recent years. This trend is largely attributed to the ubiquity of smartphones, making shopping on the go more accessible and convenient.

1. Mobile-Optimized Websites and Apps

The focus is on creating user-friendly mobile apps and websites that offer seamless shopping experiences. Progressive Web Apps (PWAs) are rising in popularity, eliminating the need for downloading and installing apps. PWAs are web applications that provide app-like features and a seamless user experience using web technologies.

2. Mobile Payment Solutions

The integration of digital wallets like Apple Pay, Google Wallet, and Samsung Pay has streamlined the checkout process, making it both faster and more secure. Additionally, "Buy now, pay later" (BNPL) services such as Afterpay and Klarna have become popular, offering flexible payment options.

3. Augmented Reality (AR) and Virtual Reality (VR)

AR and VR technologies are enhancing online shopping by allowing customers to visualize products in real-life scenarios before making a purchase. Virtual try-ons for clothing and cosmetics, as well as virtual showrooms for furniture and home décor, are gaining momentum.

Personalization and Data-Driven Shopping

Online retailers are increasingly harnessing the power of data to personalize the shopping experience, offering products and content tailored to individual preferences.

1. Recommendation Engines

E-commerce giants like Amazon have set the standard for product recommendations. Machine learning algorithms analyze past purchases and browsing history to suggest products relevant to individual tastes.

2. Customer Journey Mapping

Retailers are mapping the entire customer journey, from the initial search to post-purchase interactions. This comprehensive view helps businesses anticipate customer needs, enabling them to provide more relevant offers and support.

3. Dynamic Pricing

Dynamic pricing algorithms, driven by data analysis, adjust product prices in real-time based on demand, supply, and customer data. This means that customers may see different prices for the same product, depending on factors like location and browsing history.

Sustainable and Ethical Shopping

The sustainability and ethical shopping trend is transforming the way consumers approach online shopping. Shoppers are increasingly seeking eco-friendly and ethically sourced products.

1. Eco-Friendly Packaging

Retailers are adopting sustainable packaging options, reducing the environmental impact of shipping. Many offer the choice to opt for minimal or plastic-free packaging.

2. Transparency and Certification

Brands are increasingly transparent about their supply chain, manufacturing processes, and ethical practices. Certifications like Fair Trade, organic, and cruelty-free are prominently displayed to appeal to conscious consumers.

3. Secondhand and Thrift Shopping

The resale market is thriving, with dedicated platforms like Poshmark and ThredUp gaining popularity. Consumers are more open to buying secondhand clothing, which reduces the fashion industry's environmental footprint. It refers to the negative impact of fashion production and consumption on the environment, including factors like pollution, waste, water usage, and carbon emissions, resulting from manufacturing, transportation, and disposal of clothing and textiles.

Voice Shopping and Smart Assistants

Voice-activated shopping through smart assistants like Amazon's Alexa and Google Assistant is becoming a significant trend, simplifying the shopping process.

1. Conversational Commerce

Users can make purchases, reorder items, and inquire about product information using natural language commands. Retailers are optimizing their online stores for voice search.

2. Integration with Smart Home Devices

Smart speakers and displays are central to the connected home. Shopping can be seamlessly integrated into daily routines, from ordering groceries to restocking household essentials.

Social Commerce

Social media platforms are evolving into powerful sales channels, merging social interaction with shopping experiences.

1. Shoppable Posts

Platforms like Instagram and Pinterest have integrated shoppable features, allowing users to click on products in posts to make purchases directly through the app.

2. Influencer Marketing

Influencers play a vital role in promoting products through authentic and relatable content. Brands collaborate with influencers to reach a broader audience.

3. Live Shopping

Live streaming shopping events, featuring influencers or brand representatives, are gaining popularity. Real-time interaction with customers enhances the shopping experience.

Artificial Intelligence (AI) and Chatbots

AI is reshaping online shopping through chatbots, virtual assistants, and data-driven insights.

1. Chatbots and Virtual Assistants

AI-powered chatbots are available 24/7 to assist customers with queries, order tracking, and recommendations. They handle routine tasks, leaving human customer service representatives to address complex issues.

2. Inventory Management

AI algorithms predict demand and optimize inventory levels, reducing overstocking and understocking issues. This benefits both retailers and customers.

3. Visual Search

AI-powered visual search allows users to upload images to find similar products, simplifying the search process and making product discovery more interactive.

The Rise of Subscription Services

Subscription-based models are gaining ground across various industries, reshaping customer loyalty and retention.

1. Subscription Boxes

Subscription boxes are a recurring service where subscribers receive curated packages of products, often on a monthly basis, tailored to their interests or needs, and can encompass a wide range of goods, from cosmetics to snacks, delivered to their door. Customers receive curated boxes of products regularly, introducing them to new items they might not have discovered otherwise. This model encourages brand loyalty and recurring revenue for retailers.

2. Auto-Replenishment

Retailers offer auto-replenishment options for consumable goods like toiletries, pet food, and cleaning supplies. Subscribers enjoy the convenience of automated deliveries.

Same-Day and Instant Delivery

Consumers expect rapid delivery, and retailers are working to meet these high expectations.

1. Same-Day Delivery

Retailers are partnering with delivery services to provide same-day delivery in select areas, a significant selling point for online shoppers.

2. Instant and Ultra-Fast Delivery

Some retailers are experimenting with instant or ultra-fast delivery, often utilizing drone or autonomous vehicle technology. *Autonomous vehicle technology* refers to systems and technologies that enable self-driving or driverless vehicles to operate without human intervention by utilizing sensors, cameras, artificial intelligence, and various algorithms to navigate and control the vehicle safely. This could revolutionize the speed of e-commerce delivery.

Augmented Reality (AR) and Virtual Reality (VR)

AR and VR are creating immersive shopping experiences that could reshape online retail.

1. Virtual Showrooms

Retailers are developing VR showrooms where customers can explore products in a 3D environment. This technology provides an engaging and informative shopping experience.

2. AR for Home Try-Ons

AR apps enable customers to "try on" products like clothing and accessories in real time using their smartphones. This reduces uncertainty about how a product will look and fit.

The Role of Big Data and Analytics

Data analytics is fundamental to modern online shopping, influencing inventory management, personalized marketing, and fraud detection.

1. Inventory Management

Advanced analytics tools help retailers optimize inventory, reducing waste and costs. Real-time data analysis ensures that products are in stock when customers want them.

2. Personalized Marketing

Data-driven insights enable retailers to create highly targeted marketing campaigns, minimizing ad spend wastage and maximizing ROI (Return on Investment, a financial metric used to evaluate the profitability or effectiveness of an investment or business endeavor by comparing the gain or loss relative to the cost of the investment, typically expressed as a percentage).

3. Fraud Detection

Big data analytics and AI are used to detect and prevent fraudulent transactions, protecting retailers and customers from cyber threats.

Conclusion

Online shopping is an ever-evolving realm, shaped by technological innovation and shifting consumer preferences. The trends discussed in this article, including M-Commerce, personalization, sustainability, voice shopping, social commerce, AI, subscriptions, fast delivery, and AR/VR, are reshaping the future of e-commerce.

For consumers, these trends offer unparalleled convenience and choice, while for retailers, they present both challenges and opportunities. Staying ahead in the world of online shopping requires adaptability, customer-centric strategies, and a commitment to innovation. As technology continues to advance and consumer expectations evolve, the journey through the online shopping landscape promises to be an exciting one, offering a plethora of options and experiences for all.

Introduction

The retail landscape is evolving at an unprecedented pace, driven by the surge of online shopping. With the convenience of e-commerce, consumers have shifted towards digital platforms, redefining the way they shop. As online shopping continues to gain prominence, traditional brick-and-mortar stores are facing new challenges. However, these challenges have also led to remarkable innovations within the offline shopping experience. This article explores the creative ways in which physical stores are adapting and innovating to stay relevant in an increasingly digital world.

Immersive In-Store Experiences

In response to the convenience and accessibility of online shopping, physical stores have turned to creating immersive shopping experiences that go beyond merely purchasing products. This innovation has proven to be a game-changer, making shopping a memorable event rather than a mundane chore.

1. Augmented Reality (AR) and Virtual Reality (VR)

One of the most remarkable advancements in in-store experiences is the integration of AR and VR technologies. Customers can use AR apps on their smartphones to visualize how furniture or clothing would look in their own homes. Similarly, VR headsets offer immersive experiences, such as trying out new video games or virtually exploring travel destinations, all within the store.

These technologies add a layer of excitement and interactivity that online shopping simply can't replicate.

2. Interactive Displays

Many retailers have embraced interactive displays and touchscreens to engage shoppers. These displays provide detailed product information, customer reviews, and style suggestions, enhancing the shopping experience. Interactive mirrors in clothing stores, for instance, can show different colors and styles without the need for changing rooms. *Interactive mirrors* are innovative displays that incorporate technology such as cameras, sensors, and touch-sensitive surfaces to enable users to interact with their own reflection or view digital content superimposed on the mirror's surface, providing information, entertainment, or augmented reality experiences.

Personalization and Customer Engagement

Online retailers are known for their sophisticated recommendation algorithms that cater to individual preferences. Physical stores are now striving to replicate this personalization and create a more intimate shopping environment.

1. Customer Data Analysis

Brick-and-mortar stores are harnessing the power of customer data to gain insights into shopping behaviors and preferences. With loyalty programs, customer feedback, and in-store tracking, retailers can provide tailored offers and recommendations. This not only boosts sales but also strengthens the relationship between the store and the customer.

2. Beacons and Location-Based Services

Beacons, small Bluetooth devices placed strategically throughout the store, can send personalized offers and recommendations to customers' smartphones as they browse the aisles. Location-based services, such as geofencing, are used to offer exclusive discounts when customers are near a particular store. These innovations are helping retailers connect with their customers on a more personal level, mirroring the advantages of online shopping.

Seamless Omnichannel Integration

Omnichannel is a retail and marketing strategy that provides a seamless and integrated shopping experience for customers across various channels and platforms, such as physical stores, online stores, mobile apps, and more, allowing them to interact with a brand or business consistently and conveniently. While online shopping is often celebrated for its convenience, physical stores are increasingly capitalizing on the benefits of an omnichannel approach. This strategy bridges the gap between offline and online shopping, allowing customers to switch between channels seamlessly.

1. Click-and-Collect

Many retailers now offer a click-and-collect service, enabling customers to browse and purchase products online, and then pick them up at a nearby store. This is not only convenient for shoppers but also drives foot traffic into physical stores.

2. In-Store Pickup Lockers

In-store pickup lockers are another innovative solution that merges online and offline shopping. Customers can order products online and pick them up from lockers installed in physical stores. This convenience blurs the lines between traditional and online shopping, providing a new level of flexibility.

Sustainable Practices

As consumers become more conscious of their environmental impact, retailers are taking steps to incorporate sustainable practices into their offline operations. Sustainability is a growing trend in the retail industry, making it crucial for physical stores to innovate in this area.

1. Eco-Friendly Store Design

Retailers are redesigning their stores with a focus on sustainability. This includes using eco-friendly building materials, energy-efficient lighting, and innovative designs that reduce waste and carbon footprints.

2. Sustainable Product Lines

Many stores are offering eco-friendly and ethically sourced product lines. These products appeal to environmentally conscious customers and contribute to a positive brand image.

Smart Store Technologies

The integration of technology in physical stores is another area where offline retailers are innovating. This not only enhances the customer experience but also helps streamline operations and improve efficiency.

1. RFID Technology

Radio-frequency identification (RFID) technology is used to track inventory in real-time. This ensures that products are always available, reduces the chances of stockouts, and enhances overall customer satisfaction.

2. Self-Checkout Kiosks

Self-checkout kiosks have become more prevalent in physical stores, reducing wait times and providing an efficient shopping experience. Customers can scan and pay for their items without the need for a cashier, mimicking the convenience of online shopping.

Community and Social Engagement

In an attempt to provide value beyond products, physical stores are fostering a sense of community and social engagement among their customers. This not only attracts foot traffic but also strengthens brand loyalty.

1. Workshops and Events

Many retailers host workshops, classes, and events within their stores. These can range from cooking classes at a grocery store to book clubs at a bookstore. Such events encourage customers to not only shop but also spend time in the store.

2. Social Media Integration

Retailers are actively engaging with customers on social media, allowing them to share their in-store experiences and products they love. This creates a sense of community and word-of-mouth marketing, which is invaluable in the digital age.

Conclusion

The world of offline shopping is far from obsolete, despite the growth of online retail. In fact, traditional brick-and-mortar stores are adapting and innovating in response to online competition. The key to their survival lies in providing unique, immersive, and personalized shopping experiences that cater to the evolving needs of consumers. The innovations discussed in this article showcase the resilience and ingenuity of physical retailers, ensuring that offline shopping remains an exciting and relevant part of the retail landscape. While the competition between offline and online shopping continues, it is the consumers who ultimately benefit from the multitude of options and innovations available to them.

Introduction

In today's digital age, the landscape of retail has undergone a profound transformation. With the advent of e-commerce, the traditional brick-and-mortar retail experience has faced unprecedented challenges. Consumers now have the option to shop from the comfort of their homes, making online shopping a convenient and attractive alternative. However, the physical retail store still holds a unique and enduring appeal. In this article, we will explore the advantages and disadvantages of shopping in physical stores, highlighting the enduring value they bring to the retail landscape.

Advantages of Brick-and-Mortar Retail

1. Tangible Experience

One of the most significant advantages of shopping in physical stores is the tangible experience it offers. Customers have the opportunity to see, touch, and try on products before making a purchase. This sensory engagement provides a level of satisfaction and assurance that online shopping cannot replicate. For instance, when shopping for clothing, customers can feel the fabric, assess the fit, and see how a particular item complements their style.

2. Instant Gratification

Physical stores offer instant gratification. When you shop in a brick-and-mortar store, you can walk out with your purchase in hand, avoiding the anticipation and delays associated with online shipping. This immediacy is especially appealing for shoppers who want their products right away.

3. Personalized Assistance

In physical stores, customers have access to knowledgeable sales associates who can offer expert advice, answer questions, and provide recommendations. This personalized assistance can be particularly valuable when purchasing complex or high-value items, such as electronics or luxury goods. It also enhances the overall shopping experience and can foster customer loyalty.

4. Social Interaction

Shopping in a physical store can be a social experience. Friends or family members can accompany you, providing an opportunity for shared activities and bonding. Additionally, in-store events, such as product launches or promotional events, can further enhance the social aspect of shopping. These interactions are often difficult to replicate in the online shopping environment.

5. Try Before You Buy

Physical stores offer the invaluable advantage of "try before you buy". Shoppers can test products to ensure they meet their expectations. This is especially important for items such as cosmetics, perfumes, and electronics, where individual preferences play a significant role. The ability to test products in-store can reduce the likelihood of returns and customer dissatisfaction.

6. Immediate Returns and Exchanges

In the event of a faulty or unsatisfactory purchase, physical stores facilitate immediate returns and exchanges. Customers can address any issues face-to-face with the store's staff, making the process more efficient and less frustrating than dealing with online customer service. This contributes to a higher level of customer trust and satisfaction.

Disadvantages of Brick-and-Mortar Retail

1. Limited Convenience

While physical stores provide an immersive shopping experience, they may lack the convenience offered by online shopping. Customers must invest time and effort to visit a store, potentially dealing with traffic, parking, and crowded spaces. This can be a significant deterrent for those seeking a quick and hassle-free shopping experience.

2. Limited Selection

Physical stores have limited shelf space, which can lead to a more restricted selection of products compared to their online counterparts. If you are looking for a specific item or a wide range of choices, an online retailer often offers a more comprehensive inventory. This limitation in selection is a significant drawback for many shoppers.

3. Fixed Operating Hours

Physical stores have fixed operating hours, which may not align with the schedules of all potential customers. This can be a hindrance for individuals with busy lifestyles or unconventional work hours who prefer to shop outside regular business hours. Online shopping, in contrast, is available 24/7, accommodating a broader range of schedules.

4. Competitive Pricing

Online retailers often have lower overhead costs compared to physical stores, allowing them to offer competitive pricing and discounts. Price-conscious consumers are drawn to online shopping for the potential cost savings. Physical stores must contend with higher operational expenses, which may lead to higher prices on certain items.

5. Limited Accessibility

Not all consumers have easy access to physical stores, particularly in rural or remote areas. For those with limited mobility or transportation options, the convenience of online shopping can be a lifeline. e-commerce platforms provide a way for individuals who might not otherwise have access to certain products to make purchases.

6. Impersonal Checkout

While physical stores offer personalized assistance, the checkout process can often be impersonal and time-consuming. Waiting in line and dealing with cashiers can be a source of frustration, especially during peak shopping seasons. Online shopping streamlines the checkout process, making it more efficient and user-friendly.

The Future of Brick-and-Mortar Retail

As e-commerce continues to grow and evolve, the future of brick-and-mortar retail remains a topic of discussion. To remain competitive and relevant, physical stores are adapting and innovating in various ways.

1. Enhanced In-Store Technology

Many physical retailers are investing in technology to improve the in-store experience. This includes implementing self-checkout kiosks, augmented reality mirrors for trying on clothing virtually, and interactive displays that provide additional product information. These technological advancements bridge the gap between online and offline shopping, making physical stores more appealing.

2. Click-and-Collect Services

Retailers are embracing the concept of "click-and-collect" services, allowing customers to browse and purchase products online and then pick them up at a nearby store. This hybrid approach combines the convenience of online shopping with the immediate gratification of in-store pickup.

3. Unique In-Store Experiences

To differentiate themselves from online competitors, physical stores are focusing on creating unique and immersive shopping experiences. This can include in-store events, live demonstrations, and interactive displays that engage and entertain customers, turning shopping into an event rather than a chore.

4. Sustainable Practices

Sustainability is an increasingly important consideration for consumers. Physical retailers are taking steps to reduce their environmental footprint by implementing eco-friendly practices, such as reducing plastic packaging, using renewable energy sources, and encouraging the recycling of old products.

5. Community Engagement

Physical stores can become central hubs in their communities, hosting local events, supporting charities, and creating a sense of belonging. This sense of community engagement can foster customer loyalty and bring people into stores not just for shopping but for the overall experience.

Conclusion

The world of retail is a dynamic and evolving landscape, with both online and offline shopping options offering distinct advantages and disadvantages. The brick-and-mortar retail experience continues to hold a unique appeal for consumers who seek tangible experiences, instant gratification, and personalized assistance. It also provides opportunities for social interaction and the ability to try products before purchase.

However, physical stores face challenges, including limited convenience, fixed operating hours, and the competitive pricing offered by online retailers. Despite these drawbacks, many brick-and-mortar retailers are adapting to the changing retail landscape by incorporating technology, offering click-and-collect services, creating unique in-store experiences, and embracing sustainability.

In the end, the future of physical retail will depend on the ability of brick-and-mortar stores to continue innovating and providing value to consumers. By combining the strengths of the physical and digital shopping experiences, retailers can create a retail landscape that seamlessly integrates both worlds, offering customers the best of both online and offline shopping.

Introduction

In the ever-evolving landscape of retail, businesses are constantly seeking innovative ways to meet the changing demands of consumers. The lines between offline and online shopping experiences are blurring, giving rise to a retail strategy known as omni-channel retailing. This approach leverages the strengths of both physical stores and e-commerce to create a seamless customer journey. In the following article, we will delve into the concept of omni-channel retailing, discussing its importance in the modern retail environment and the ways in which it enhances the customer experience.

Defining Omni-Channel Retailing

Omni-channel retailing is a strategy that centers around creating a unified shopping experience for customers, whether they are in-store or online. The key principle behind this approach is to break down the traditional silos between brick-and-mortar and e-commerce channels, enabling consumers to transition seamlessly between them. This integration brings numerous benefits to both retailers and consumers, making it a crucial element in modern retail strategies.

The Importance of a Seamless Customer Journey

1. Consumer Expectations

In today's digital age, consumers have grown accustomed to convenience, personalization, and instant gratification. They expect to engage with brands on their own terms, with the ability to browse, purchase, and receive products in a manner that suits their preferences. Omni-channel retailing acknowledges and caters to these evolving customer expectations, ensuring a shopping experience that is consistent and frictionless.

2. Enhanced Customer Loyalty

One of the primary advantages of omni-channel retailing is the potential for enhanced customer loyalty. When consumers experience a brand consistently across different channels, they are more likely to develop a deep connection with it. This loyalty is fostered through a sense of trust and reliability, as customers know they can rely on the brand to provide a high-quality experience, regardless of how and where they shop.

3. Data-Driven Insights

Omni-channel retailing allows retailers to gather a wealth of data on customer behavior. This data can be harnessed to gain insights into shopping patterns, preferences, and trends. With a holistic view of their customers, businesses can tailor their marketing, product offerings, and promotions more effectively, resulting in increased sales and customer satisfaction.

Seamless Integration of Offline and Online Shopping Experiences

1. Unified Inventory

One of the cornerstones of omni-channel retailing is the integration of inventory across various sales channels. This means that customers can easily check product availability, make purchases online and pick up or return items in-store.

This level of flexibility not only benefits customers but also reduces inventory costs and streamlines the supply chain for retailers.

2. Cross-Channel Consistency

Creating a seamless customer journey requires consistent branding and messaging across all channels. A customer should feel the same ambiance and recognition when walking into a physical store as they do when browsing a retailer's website. This consistency reinforces the brand's identity and helps build trust and recognition among consumers.

3. Personalization

Online shopping allows for sophisticated personalization through data analysis and algorithms. Retailers can use this data to recommend products to customers based on their previous purchases and preferences. Omni-channel retailing extends this personalization to the in-store experience by using customer data to provide tailored assistance and offers when a customer visits a physical location.

4. Flexible Fulfillment Options

Omni-channel retailing offers customers a variety of fulfillment options, such as buy online, pick up in-store (BOPIS), curbside (area immediately adjacent to the curb or edge of a road or parking lot) pickup, and same-day delivery. This flexibility accommodates a range of customer needs and preferences, whether they want instant gratification or the convenience of online shopping with a physical pickup location.

Successful Examples of Omni-Channel Retailing

Several companies have successfully implemented omni-channel strategies to enhance their customers' shopping experiences. Let's explore a few examples:

1. Starbucks

Starbucks has taken a customer-centric approach by integrating its mobile app with in-store experiences. Customers can order their favorite coffee in advance and pay through the app, saving time and avoiding long lines. Starbucks has also implemented a rewards program that works seamlessly across channels, making it a prime example of omni-channel success.

2. Sephora

Sephora has transformed its stores into beauty havens by incorporating digital experiences. Customers can use in-store technology to virtually try on makeup, access personalized product recommendations, and accumulate loyalty points that apply both online and in-store. This innovative approach fosters a unique and interactive shopping experience.

3. Best Buy

Best Buy has capitalized on the showrooming trend, where customers visit physical stores to view products before making online purchases. The retailer adapted by offering price matching, expert advice from in-store associates, and a consistent online shopping experience, effectively bridging the gap between in-store and online shopping.

Challenges in Implementing Omni-Channel Retailing

While omni-channel retailing offers numerous advantages, it is not without its challenges.

1. Technology Integration

Integrating various technologies and platforms across channels can be complex and costly. Retailers must invest in robust systems that enable real-time inventory management, personalized marketing, and a seamless customer experience.

2. Data Security

Handling customer data across multiple channels necessitates a robust approach to data security and privacy. Retailers must ensure that sensitive customer information is protected from potential breaches and adhere to data protection regulations.

3. Employee Training

To provide a consistent omni-channel experience, employees must be trained to work with various technologies and interact with customers in ways that align with the brand's values and mission.

4. Organizational Alignment

Retailers often have to restructure their organizations to break down silos between online and offline channels. This might involve changes in leadership, communication, and company culture to foster a unified vision.

The Future of Omni-Channel Retailing

Omni-channel retailing is not a passing trend; it's the future of retail. As technology continues to advance and consumer expectations evolve, retailers must adapt to stay competitive. The future of omni-channel retailing holds the promise of even more innovation.

1. Augmented Reality (AR) and Virtual Reality (VR)

AR and VR technologies are poised to revolutionize the way customers experience products both online and in-store. Customers will be able to virtually try on clothing, visualize furniture in their homes, and explore products in immersive ways, enhancing the omni-channel experience.

2. Voice Commerce

Voice-activated devices like smart speakers are becoming an integral part of the omni-channel experience. Customers can make purchases, check product availability, and get product recommendations through voice commands.

3. Artificial Intelligence (AI)

AI will continue to play a significant role in personalizing the shopping experience. AI-powered chatbots and virtual shopping assistants will be able to engage with customers, answer questions, and make recommendations, whether online or in-store.

Conclusion

Omni-channel retailing is more than just a buzzword; it's a strategic imperative for retailers looking to thrive in the digital age. The importance of providing a seamless customer journey that integrates both offline and online shopping experiences cannot be overstated. Consumers expect a consistent brand experience, personalization, and the flexibility to shop how and where they want. Successful omni-channel retailing not only meets these expectations but also offers a competitive advantage, fosters customer loyalty, and generates valuable data-driven insights. As the retail landscape continues to evolve, businesses that embrace omni-channel retailing will be well-positioned to navigate the world of offline and online shopping successfully.

Introduction

The world of shopping has undergone a significant transformation over the past few decades, transitioning from traditional brick-and-mortar stores to a seamless fusion of offline and online experiences. At the heart of this transformation lies the omnipresent smartphone and the myriad shopping apps that have reshaped the way we shop. In this article, we will delve into the role of smartphones and shopping apps in the modern shopping experience, exploring their impact on consumer behavior, convenience, and the retail industry as a whole.

The Rise of Mobile Shopping

The rapid adoption of smartphones has been nothing short of revolutionary in the world of retail. With the advancement of technology and the widespread availability of high-speed internet, mobile shopping has become increasingly popular. Consumers now have the world's largest shopping mall in their pockets, available 24/7. As a result, shopping has evolved from a time-consuming and location-bound activity to a quick and convenient process that can be done from anywhere.

1. The Convenience Factor

Smartphones have redefined convenience in shopping. Whether you're on your daily commute, waiting for a friend, or just relaxing at home, you can access your favorite shopping apps with a few taps. This convenience has reshaped consumer behavior, making impromptu (without advance preparation or planning) and spontaneous shopping more common than ever before. The ability to shop anytime, anywhere has disrupted the traditional shopping schedule and made it more adaptable to our busy lives.

2. Enhanced Personalization

Shopping apps are designed to gather and analyze user data, allowing for tailored recommendations and a highly personalized shopping experience. This level of personalization is often unattainable in physical stores. Mobile apps can offer product suggestions based on a user's past purchases, browsing history, and preferences, thereby increasing the chances of making a sale. The ability to provide a more personalized shopping experience has played a pivotal role in the success of mobile shopping.

3. Accessibility and Inclusivity

Mobile shopping apps have contributed to making the world of retail more inclusive. They provide features that cater to individuals with disabilities, making it easier for them to shop independently. Features such as voice commands, screen readers, and adjustable font sizes enhance the shopping experience for everyone, regardless of physical abilities. Furthermore, mobile apps often offer multilingual support, opening up a world of shopping opportunities for a diverse global audience.

The Pervasiveness of Shopping Apps

Shopping apps have become a cornerstone of the mobile shopping experience. These apps encompass a wide range of retailers, from global e-commerce giants to local boutique stores. The variety of available shopping apps is staggering, and consumers can find apps for virtually any product or service they desire.

1. Retail Giants Leading the Way

E-commerce giants like Amazon, Alibaba, and eBay have set the standard for shopping apps. They offer extensive product catalogs, one-click purchasing, and swift delivery options. These platforms have disrupted traditional retail models and redefined customer expectations, setting a high bar for other shopping apps to follow.

2. Niche and Specialty Apps

Beyond the retail giants, niche and specialty shopping apps have found their place in the market. Apps like Etsy, which caters to handmade and vintage products, or Zillow, which specializes in real estate listings, have created unique ecosystems for consumers with specific needs and interests. These apps demonstrate the adaptability of the mobile shopping landscape.

3. Social Commerce

Social media platforms like Instagram and Facebook have ventured into the shopping app space, integrating e-commerce into their core functionalities. This development has made the shopping experience seamless for users, who can now explore and purchase products without leaving their favorite social media apps. Social commerce blurs the lines between social interaction and shopping, creating a holistic experience.

Transforming Consumer Behavior

The widespread use of smartphones and shopping apps has not only made shopping more convenient but has also reshaped consumer behavior and expectations.

1. Showrooming and Webrooming

Showrooming, the practice of examining products in a physical store and then purchasing them online, and webrooming, where consumers research products online and then make in-store purchases, have become common consumer practices. Shopping apps enable this behavior by providing easy access to product information, user reviews, and price comparisons.

2. Impulse Buying

The ease of mobile shopping and the convenience of shopping apps have contributed to an increase in impulse buying. With a few taps on the screen, consumers can make quick purchasing decisions, sometimes driven by discounts, limited-time offers, or personalized recommendations. Shopping apps capitalize on this consumer behavior by offering limited-time deals and flash sales.

3. Price Sensitivity

Mobile shopping apps often provide price comparison tools, enabling consumers to find the best deals and discounts. This heightened price sensitivity has made retailers more competitive, as consumers can easily compare prices and choose the most cost-effective option. As a result, retailers are forced to adapt and offer competitive pricing.

The Retail Industry's Response

The retail industry has undergone significant changes in response to the mobile shopping revolution. While many traditional retailers have struggled to keep pace, others have embraced technology to enhance the shopping experience.

1. Omni-Channel Strategies

To stay relevant in the age of mobile shopping, many brick-and-mortar retailers have adopted omni-channel strategies. These strategies involve integrating online and offline channels to provide a seamless shopping experience. Retailers have developed their mobile apps, allowing customers to make purchases, check inventory, and receive personalized promotions both in-store and online. Additionally, buy-online-pick-up-in-store (BOPIS) options have gained popularity, offering the convenience of online shopping with the immediacy of in-store pickup.

2. Augmented Reality (AR) and Virtual Reality (VR)

The retail industry has begun to experiment with AR and VR technologies to enhance the shopping experience. AR apps enable customers to visualize products in their real environment before making a purchase, while VR can create immersive virtual shopping experiences. These technologies bridge the gap between the online and offline worlds and offer customers a more engaging and interactive way to shop.

3. Data Analytics and Customer Insights

Retailers are increasingly relying on data analytics to gain deeper insights into customer behavior. Shopping apps collect vast amounts of data, from browsing history to purchase patterns, enabling retailers to make informed decisions about product offerings, pricing, and marketing strategies. By leveraging data analytics, retailers can create a more personalized and relevant shopping experience for their customers.

Challenges and Concerns

Despite the numerous advantages of mobile shopping and shopping apps, several challenges and concerns have emerged.

1. Security and Privacy

As more personal and financial data is shared through mobile shopping apps, concerns about security and privacy have grown. Consumers worry about data breaches, identity theft, and the misuse of their information. Retailers must invest in robust security measures to address these concerns and build trust with their customers.

2. Screen Fatigue

The constant use of smartphones for shopping and other activities can lead to screen fatigue. Consumers may become overwhelmed by the sheer volume of information and choices available on shopping apps. This can lead to decision paralysis and a desire for a break from digital interfaces.

3. Reduced In-Store Experiences

The rise of mobile shopping and online retail can lead to a decline in traditional in-store experiences. As more consumers opt for the convenience of shopping from their smartphones, physical retailers may struggle to compete. This challenges the traditional retail model and raises questions about the future of brick-and-mortar stores.

Conclusion

Mobile shopping and shopping apps have transformed the modern shopping experience, offering unparalleled convenience, personalization, and accessibility. Smartphones and apps have redefined consumer behavior, making showrooming, webrooming, and impulse buying more prevalent. The retail industry has responded by embracing technology, implementing omni-channel strategies, and experimenting with augmented and virtual reality.

However, challenges related to security, screen fatigue, and the impact on in-store experiences must be addressed. As the world of retail continues to evolve, the role of smartphones and shopping apps will remain central, shaping the way we shop and the future of the retail industry. As consumers, retailers, and technology developers work together, we can look forward to an even more dynamic and convenient shopping landscape, where online and offline shopping seamlessly coexist.

Introduction

The advent of the internet has revolutionized the way we shop, giving birth to a new era of retail - e-commerce. E-commerce platforms have played a pivotal role in shaping the online shopping landscape, offering consumers and businesses convenient, efficient, and diverse shopping experiences. This article delves into the world of e-commerce platforms, exploring major online marketplaces and platforms, and offering insights into their significance in the realm of modern shopping.

The e-commerce Revolution

Before diving into the specifics of various e-commerce platforms, let's understand the broader context of this retail revolution.

1. The Digital Transformation of Retail

In the past few decades, the retail industry has experienced a profound digital transformation. The convenience of online shopping, coupled with evolving consumer preferences, has led to a shift in the way people make purchases. e-commerce platforms have become the primary means of shopping for a significant portion of the global population.

2. The Impact of COVID-19

The COVID-19 pandemic accelerated the shift towards online shopping, pushing even traditional retailers to establish an online presence. This crisis underscored the significance of e-commerce platforms in sustaining business continuity.

Major Online Marketplaces

Online marketplaces are platforms where multiple sellers can list their products, providing consumers with a wide array of choices.

A B2B (Business-to-Business) marketplace is an online platform where businesses sell products or services to other businesses. It facilitates transactions between manufacturers, wholesalers, distributors, and other companies. Examples include Alibaba and ThomasNet. A B2C (Business-to-Consumer) marketplace is an online platform where businesses sell products or services directly to individual consumers. It's the most common form of e-commerce and includes platforms like Amazon and eBay, where consumers can purchase items for personal use.

Let's explore some of the major online marketplaces.

1. Amazon

Amazon, the e-commerce behemoth founded by Jeff Bezos, is the world's largest online marketplace. It boasts millions of products, offering everything from books to electronics, groceries to fashion. Amazon Prime, a subscription service, provides customers with expedited shipping, access to streaming services, and exclusive deals.

2. eBay

eBay is a pioneer in the online marketplace industry, known for its auctions and a vast range of used and new items. It offers a unique shopping experience, allowing consumers to bid on items, setting it apart from other e-commerce platforms.

3. Etsy

Etsy caters to a niche market of handmade, vintage, and unique items. It's a platform where artisans and crafters can sell their products, creating a community for those seeking one-of-a-kind items.

4. Alibaba

Alibaba, the Chinese giant, is a global B2B and B2C marketplace. It connects international buyers and sellers, offering a vast array of products, with a focus on wholesale and bulk orders.

5. Walmart Marketplace

Walmart, the retail giant, has ventured into the online marketplace domain. Walmart Marketplace allows third-party sellers to reach a broader customer base, competing with platforms like Amazon.

E-commerce Platforms

While online marketplaces aggregate products from various sellers, e-commerce platforms are complete solutions for businesses to set up their online stores. Let's explore some of the most prominent e-commerce platforms.

1. Shopify

Shopify is a leading e-commerce platform known for its user-friendly interface and comprehensive features. It empowers businesses to create and manage their online stores with ease. From inventory management to customizable themes, Shopify is a versatile solution for businesses of all sizes.

2. WooCommerce

WooCommerce is a plugin for WordPress, the popular content management system. It offers a powerful e-commerce solution for businesses looking to integrate online shopping into their existing websites. WooCommerce is open-source, highly customizable, and has a strong developer community.

3. Magento

Magento, now owned by Adobe, is a robust e-commerce platform primarily aimed at larger businesses. It offers advanced features, scalability, and customization options, making it suitable for enterprises with complex e-commerce needs.

4. BigCommerce

BigCommerce is a popular e-commerce platform that provides businesses with the tools and features to create and manage online stores. It offers a range of e-commerce solutions, including website building, product catalog management, payment processing, and marketing capabilities, designed to help businesses sell products and services online.

5. Wix

Wix is a versatile website builder that includes e-commerce capabilities. It's a great choice for businesses that want to have a stunning website and sell products online. Wix offers a simple drag-and-drop interface, making it accessible to those with minimal technical skills.

The Significance of e-commerce Platforms

E-commerce platforms and online marketplaces have become integral to modern shopping for several reasons.

1. Accessibility

E-commerce platforms have made shopping accessible to everyone, irrespective of location. Customers can browse and purchase products from the comfort of their homes, eliminating the need for physical store visits.

2. Variety and Choice

Online marketplaces and e-commerce platforms offer a vast array of products. Whether you're looking for electronics, fashion, or niche items, you'll find countless choices at your fingertips.

3. Convenience

The convenience of online shopping is a major draw. Customers can shop at any time, track orders, and receive deliveries at their doorstep. This convenience is especially appealing to busy individuals.

4. Competitive Pricing

E-commerce platforms promote price transparency and competition. Shoppers can easily compare prices, read reviews, and make informed decisions about their purchases.

5. Global Reach

E-commerce platforms break down geographical barriers, allowing businesses to reach a global audience. This has opened up new opportunities for small and medium-sized enterprises (SMEs) to expand their reach.

Challenges and Opportunities

While e-commerce platforms offer numerous advantages, they also present certain challenges and opportunities for both businesses and consumers.

1. Competition

The abundance of online sellers on e-commerce platforms means intense competition. Businesses need to differentiate themselves through product quality, pricing, and marketing strategies to succeed.

2. Data Security

With the rise in online transactions, data security and privacy are paramount concerns. e-commerce platforms must invest in robust security measures to protect customer information.

3. Customer Experience

The digital shopping experience must be seamless and user-friendly. Businesses must invest in user experience (UX) design and customer support to retain and attract customers.

4. Sustainability

The environmental impact of e-commerce, including packaging and shipping, is a growing concern. E-commerce platforms have the opportunity to lead the way in adopting sustainable practices.

5. Emerging Technologies

E-commerce is continually evolving with the integration of technologies like AI, AR, and blockchain. *Blockchain* is a decentralized and distributed digital ledger technology that records transactions across multiple computers in a way that ensures the security, transparency, and immutability of data. These technologies offer new ways to enhance the online shopping experience.

The Future of E-commerce Platforms

The future of e-commerce platforms is shaped by ongoing technological advancements, changing consumer behavior, and global market dynamics.

1. Mobile Shopping

Mobile shopping is on the rise, and e-commerce platforms are adapting to this trend. User-friendly mobile apps and responsive websites are essential for reaching the growing number of mobile shoppers.

2. Personalization

Personalized shopping experiences are becoming more prevalent. e-commerce platforms are leveraging AI and data analytics to tailor product recommendations and marketing strategies to individual preferences.

3. Augmented Reality (AR)

AR is transforming the way consumers shop online. E-commerce platforms are incorporating AR features, allowing customers to visualize products in their own space before making a purchase.

4. Cross-Border Shopping

Globalization continues to shape the e-commerce landscape. Cross-border shopping is becoming easier, with platforms offering international shipping and multilingual support.

5. Sustainability Initiatives

E-commerce platforms are increasingly focusing on sustainability. They are working to reduce their environmental impact by adopting eco-friendly packaging, promoting green practices, and supporting eco-conscious brands.

Conclusion

E-commerce platforms have not only transformed the way we shop but have also reshaped the retail industry itself. They offer accessibility, convenience, and a diverse range of products to consumers, while providing businesses with the means to reach a global audience. As technology continues to advance, e-commerce platforms are poised to adapt and offer more innovative and sustainable shopping experiences. By understanding and navigating this evolving world of online shopping, consumers and businesses alike can benefit from the opportunities it presents.

In the grand narrative of retail, e-commerce platforms have played a pivotal role in authoring a new chapter. They have brought the marketplace to our screens, reshaping the way we engage with commerce, and as the world continues to evolve, these platforms will undoubtedly be at the forefront of change, ushering in new trends and possibilities in the realm of shopping.

Introduction

In today's fast-paced world, the way we shop has undergone a transformation. Whether it's strolling through a bustling mall or browsing through an online marketplace, the convenience and variety at our disposal are staggering. However, as shopping methods evolve, so do payment options. In this article, we'll explore the diverse range of payment methods and transactions, from traditional credit cards to the digital wallets that have taken the e-commerce world by storm. Understanding these options is vital for consumers, as it ensures secure and convenient shopping experiences, whether offline or online.

Traditional Payment Methods

1. Credit Cards

Credit cards are one of the oldest and most widely accepted forms of payment. They provide a revolving line of credit, allowing consumers to make purchases and repay the balance at a later date. How they work:

- ❖ Credit cards are issued by banks or financial institutions.
- ❖ Each card has a credit limit, which represents the maximum amount that can be spent.
- ❖ When making a purchase, the cardholder swipes or inserts the card into a card reader.
- ❖ The payment is authorized, and the amount is deducted from the available credit limit.

❖ Cardholders receive a monthly statement, detailing their purchases and the minimum amount due.
❖ Interest is charged on the outstanding balance if not paid in full by the due date.

2. Debit Cards

Debit cards are linked to a checking (current) or savings account, and they allow consumers to make payments directly from their account. Unlike credit cards, debit card purchases deduct the funds immediately from the associated account.

❖ Debit cards are issued by banks and linked to a checking or savings account.
❖ When making a purchase, the cardholder swipes or inserts the card or uses it for online transactions.
❖ The payment is authorized, and the amount is debited from the linked bank account.
❖ There is no need for repayment, as debit cards use the cardholder's own funds.

Emerging Digital Payment Methods

1. Digital Wallets

Digital wallets, also known as e-wallets or mobile wallets, are increasingly popular for online and offline transactions. They store payment information and offer a streamlined way to make payments. Key digital wallet providers include Apple Pay, Google Pay, PayPal, and Samsung Pay.

How digital wallets work:

❖ Users set up a digital wallet by linking their credit card, debit card, or bank account information.

- ❖ When making a payment, the user selects the digital wallet as the payment method.
- ❖ The digital wallet securely stores the payment information and generates a unique token for each transaction.
- ❖ This token is sent to the merchant for payment authorization, ensuring that the user's sensitive financial details are never exposed.
- ❖ Digital wallets often offer loyalty programs, discounts, and the ability to store various payment methods in one place.

2. Contactless Payments

Contactless payments have gained momentum due to their speed and convenience, especially in the age of COVID-19. This method involves tapping or waving a card, smartphone, or smartwatch near a contactless-enabled terminal for payment.

How contactless payments work:

- ❖ Contactless payment methods include contactless credit/debit cards, mobile wallets, and wearable devices.
- ❖ The user's payment information is stored in the chosen device.
- ❖ To make a payment, the user holds the device near a contactless-enabled point-of-sale terminal.
- ❖ The payment is authorized, and the transaction is completed within seconds.
- ❖ Security features like tokenization help protect contactless payments against fraud.

Online Payment Gateways

Online shopping has become a global phenomenon, and to cater to this, various online payment gateways have emerged. These gateways facilitate the secure processing of online transactions, bridging the gap between consumers and e-commerce platforms. Common online payment gateways include PayPal, Stripe, and Square.

How online payment gateways work:

- ❖ When a customer selects products or services online and proceeds to checkout, they are redirected to the payment gateway.
- ❖ The customer enters their payment information, which is encrypted to ensure security.
- ❖ The payment gateway processes the transaction and communicates with the customer's bank for authorization.
- ❖ Once approved, the payment gateway sends a confirmation to the online store, and the transaction is complete.
- ❖ Online payment gateways often provide options for credit cards, digital wallets, and other payment methods.

Cryptocurrency Transactions

Cryptocurrency is a relatively new player in the world of payment methods. It operates on blockchain technology, enabling secure, decentralized transactions. Bitcoin, Ethereum, and Ripple are some of the most popular cryptocurrencies.

How cryptocurrency transactions work:

- ❖ Users acquire cryptocurrency through exchanges or mining (process of validating and recording transactions on a blockchain).
- ❖ Each user has a digital wallet that stores their cryptocurrency holdings.
- ❖ To make a payment, the payer enters the recipient's cryptocurrency wallet address and the amount to be sent.
- ❖ The transaction is broadcast to the blockchain network for verification by miners.
- ❖ Once verified, the cryptocurrency is transferred to the recipient's wallet.
- ❖ Cryptocurrency transactions provide security and privacy, but they can be subject to volatility in value.

QR Code Payments

QR code payments have gained traction in recent years, simplifying transactions for both businesses and consumers. These codes contain payment information and can be scanned using a smartphone camera or a dedicated app.

How QR code payments work:

- ❖ Merchants generate a QR code containing the payment details, including the transaction amount.
- ❖ Customers use their smartphone camera to scan the QR code.
- ❖ The payment app on the customer's device processes the transaction and prompts the user to confirm.

* ❖ Upon confirmation, the payment is authorized and completed.
* ❖ QR code payments are convenient for both in-person and online transactions.

Peer-to-Peer (P2P) Payment Apps

P2P payment apps allow individuals to send money to each other instantly, making them useful for splitting bills, repaying debts, and more. Popular P2P payment apps include Venmo, Cash App, and Zelle.

How P2P payment apps work:

* ❖ Users link their bank accounts or credit/debit cards to the app.
* ❖ To send money, the user selects a recipient from their contacts or enters their email or phone number.
* ❖ The app processes the transaction and debits the sender's account.
* ❖ The recipient receives a notification and can transfer the received funds to their bank account.
* ❖ P2P payment apps often offer social features, allowing users to add notes and share payments publicly or privately.

Payment Security

Ensuring the security of payment methods is paramount for both consumers and businesses. The methods mentioned above have various security measures in place, but it's essential to take additional precautions.

* ❖ Regularly monitor bank and credit card statements for unauthorized transactions.

- ❖ Use strong, unique passwords and enable two-factor authentication for online payment accounts.
- ❖ Keep digital wallets and mobile devices secure with passcodes, biometric authentication, or PINs.
- ❖ Beware of phishing scams and only enter payment information on reputable websites and apps.
- ❖ Regularly update and patch your devices and apps to protect against security vulnerabilities.

Conclusion

The world of payment methods and transactions has evolved dramatically in recent years, offering consumers an array of choices for both online and offline shopping. From traditional credit and debit cards to emerging digital payment methods like digital wallets and cryptocurrencies, understanding these options is crucial for navigating the world of modern commerce.

Each payment method has its own set of advantages and considerations. Credit cards offer flexibility and credit-building opportunities but can lead to debt if not managed responsibly. Debit cards provide a direct link to personal funds, eliminating the risk of debt but offering fewer perks. Digital wallets and contactless payments are convenient and secure, making them ideal for both in-store and online transactions. Online payment gateways have revolutionized e-commerce, ensuring secure and efficient transactions. Cryptocurrency transactions offer privacy and security, but their value can be volatile. QR code payments simplify the transaction process, and P2P payment apps make it easy to transfer money between individuals.

Regardless of the method chosen, security should always be a top priority. Vigilance, strong passwords, and awareness of potential scams are essential for safe and secure payments. By understanding these various payment methods and taking appropriate precautions, consumers can confidently navigate the world of offline and online shopping, enjoying the convenience and security that modern technology provides.

Introduction

The rapid growth of e-commerce has transformed the way we shop, making it more convenient and accessible than ever before. With just a few clicks, consumers can explore a world of products and services from the comfort of their own homes. However, as the e-commerce landscape has expanded, so too have concerns about security and privacy. In a world where personal and financial information is shared online, the importance of trust cannot be overstated. This article delves into the critical aspects of e-commerce security and data protection, highlighting their significance in building trust with online shoppers.

The Evolution of E-Commerce

E-commerce, or electronic commerce, refers to the buying and selling of goods and services over the internet. It has evolved significantly over the past few decades. From the early days of online shopping with limited product offerings and rudimentary payment systems, it has grown into a massive global industry, encompassing a vast array of products and services. The convenience and accessibility of e-commerce have made it a preferred shopping method for millions of people worldwide.

The Role of Trust in E-Commerce

Trust is a fundamental factor in any commercial transaction, whether it occurs in a physical store or online. In e-commerce, establishing trust is particularly crucial because shoppers must entrust their personal and financial information to online retailers. This trust can be built through various means, with security and data protection being paramount.

E-commerce Security

1. Authentication and Authorization

Authentication and authorization are the first line of defense in e-commerce security. Authentication ensures that users are who they claim to be, while authorization defines what actions they are allowed to perform within a system. Usernames and passwords are commonly used for authentication, and multi-factor authentication (MFA) has become increasingly popular for added security. MFA requires users to provide two or more forms of authentication, such as a password and a unique code sent to their mobile device.

2. Secure Sockets Layer (SSL) and Transport Layer Security (TLS)

SSL and TLS are cryptographic protocols that establish secure connections between a user's browser and a website's server. These protocols encrypt data transferred between the two, making it extremely difficult for hackers to intercept and decipher sensitive information like credit card details. Shoppers can identify secure connections by looking for "https://" and a padlock icon in the browser's address bar.

3. Secure Payment Gateways

Payment gateways are intermediaries that facilitate the transfer of funds between the shopper, the online retailer, and the financial institution. These gateways employ advanced security measures to safeguard payment information. The use of well-known and trusted payment gateways can reassure shoppers that their financial data is handled with care.

Data Protection in E-Commerce

1. Data Encryption

Data encryption is a key component of data protection. It involves encoding sensitive information so that only authorized parties can access it. In e-commerce, encryption is applied not only during transactions but also when storing customer data. This ensures that even if a data breach occurs, the stolen information remains indecipherable to cybercriminals.

2. Data Privacy Regulations

Various data privacy regulations, such as the General Data Protection Regulation (GDPR) in Europe and the California Consumer Privacy Act (CCPA) in the United States, have been implemented to protect consumers' personal data. These regulations require online retailers to be transparent about how they collect and use customer data, and to provide consumers with the option to control the information they share.

3. Secure Data Storage

Online retailers must store customer data securely to prevent data breaches and protect sensitive information. This involves using robust security measures, including firewalls and intrusion detection systems. Regular security audits and updates are essential to ensure the ongoing protection of stored data.

Building Trust through Transparency

Transparency plays a critical role in building trust between online retailers and shoppers. When consumers are well-informed about how their data is handled and the security measures in place, they are more likely to feel confident in making online purchases. Retailers can achieve this by:

1. Privacy Policies

Maintaining clear and comprehensive privacy policies that explain how customer data is collected, used, and protected. It should also outline customers' rights regarding their data.

2. Security Certifications

Displaying security certifications, such as the Payment Card Industry Data Security Standard (PCI DSS) compliance or SSL/TLS certificates, on the website can instill confidence in shoppers. These certifications are awarded to businesses that meet specific security standards.

3. Customer Support and Communication

Offering responsive customer support and clear communication channels can help address shoppers' concerns promptly. A responsive support team can provide assistance in the event of security or privacy issues, reassuring customers that their needs are taken seriously.

The Cost of Data Breaches

Data breaches can have significant financial and reputational consequences for e-commerce businesses. When sensitive information is compromised, it can result in legal consequences, loss of customer trust, and a damaged brand reputation. To mitigate these risks, it is essential for online retailers to invest in robust security measures and data protection protocols.

Challenges in E-commerce Security and Privacy

The ever-evolving landscape of cybersecurity presents continuous challenges for e-commerce businesses. Some of the notable challenges include:

1. Phishing Attacks

Phishing attacks involve tricking individuals into revealing their personal information, often through deceptive emails or websites that appear legitimate. Online retailers must educate their customers about recognizing and avoiding phishing attempts.

2. Evolving Cyber Threats

Cyber threats are constantly evolving, with hackers finding new ways to exploit vulnerabilities. Online retailers must stay up-to-date with the latest security measures to protect against emerging threats.

3. Regulatory Compliance

Complying with various data privacy regulations, which can vary by region and change over time, is a continuous challenge. Online retailers must adapt their practices to remain compliant with evolving laws.

Case Study: The Importance of Trust in E-Commerce

To illustrate the significance of trust in e-commerce, consider the case of a major online retailer that suffered a data breach. In 2013, Target, one of the largest retailers in the United States, experienced a high-profile data breach. Cybercriminals gained access to customer data, compromising the credit card information of over 40 million shoppers.

The breach not only resulted in significant financial losses for Target but also severely damaged its reputation. Customers lost trust in the retailer, and many were hesitant to shop there again. This incident highlights the devastating consequences of failing to protect customer data and the critical role of trust in e-commerce.

Conclusion

E-commerce has revolutionized the way we shop, offering unprecedented convenience and access to a vast array of products and services. However, the success of online shopping hinges on trust. Shoppers must feel confident that their personal and financial information is secure, and their privacy is respected. E-commerce security and data protection are the cornerstones of building and maintaining this trust.

Online retailers must invest in robust security measures, ensure data protection, and be transparent about their practices. Building trust in the digital marketplace is not just a matter of good business ethics; it's a necessity for the continued success of e-commerce.

As the e-commerce landscape continues to evolve, so too will the challenges and threats to security and privacy. Online retailers must remain vigilant, adapt to changing circumstances, and prioritize the protection of customer data. In doing so, they will not only foster trust but also contribute to the continued growth and success of the e-commerce industry.

Introduction

In the age of digital transformation, social media has become an integral part of our lives, significantly influencing our behaviors and choices, particularly in the realm of shopping. The way consumers browse, discover, and purchase products and services has been revolutionized by platforms like Facebook, Instagram, Twitter, and Pinterest. This article explores the multifaceted impact of social media on shopping, delving into how it shapes consumer behavior, influences shopping trends, and bridges the gap between offline and online shopping.

The Evolution of Social Media and Shopping

The inception of social media platforms brought forth a new era of connectivity and information sharing. Initially, these platforms were designed for interpersonal communication, but they have since evolved into powerful marketing and shopping tools. With billions of active users, they have the potential to transform the way we shop.

The Influence of Social Media on Consumer Behavior

1. Building Trust and Credibility

Social media is a platform where consumers engage with brands, read reviews, and build trust. Positive feedback and a strong online presence are essential for businesses in building credibility and trustworthiness. Today's shoppers often turn to social media for recommendations and endorsements from friends, family, and influencers, and these endorsements have a profound impact on their choices.

2. Emotional Connection

Social media allows brands to create emotional connections with their audience. Content that evokes emotions, such as joy, nostalgia, or excitement, can result in higher engagement and greater brand loyalty. Emotional branding on social media often leads to consumers associating a positive sentiment with a particular product or brand.

3. FOMO (Fear of Missing Out)

The "Fear of Missing Out" is a psychological trigger amplified by social media. When consumers see their peers engaging with certain products or trends, they often feel compelled to join in to avoid feeling left out. Social media promotes trends and product launches, making it easier for businesses to leverage this phenomenon.

Shaping Shopping Trends

1. Influencer Marketing

One of the most significant impacts of social media on shopping is the rise of influencer marketing. Influencers are individuals who have amassed a significant following on platforms like Instagram, YouTube, and TikTok. Brands partner with these influencers to promote their products, relying on their trust and authority with their followers. The influencer marketing industry has grown exponentially and plays a substantial role in shaping shopping trends.

2. Viral Challenges and Trends

Social media platforms are breeding grounds for viral challenges and trends that can skyrocket product sales. Challenges like the "Ice Bucket Challenge" or trends like "sourdough bread baking" have led to a surge in the demand for specific products. Businesses that can align their offerings with these trends can reap significant rewards.

3. User-Generated Content

User-generated content, including reviews, unboxing videos, and testimonials, significantly influences shopping trends. *Unboxing videos* are online videos where individuals open and reveal the contents of a product's packaging, providing a visual and often detailed narration of their first impressions and experiences with the product. These videos are often used for reviews, demonstrations, or simply entertainment. Consumers trust their peers more than traditional advertising, and these authentic forms of content play a crucial role in shaping buying decisions. Businesses often encourage customers to share their experiences on social media, thereby influencing the choices of others.

Bridging the Gap Between Offline and Online Shopping

1. Social Commerce

Social commerce has emerged as a powerful bridge between offline and online shopping. Platforms like Facebook, Instagram, and Pinterest have integrated shopping features directly into their interfaces. Users can now discover, browse, and purchase products without leaving the platform. This seamless experience has led to a surge in online sales and has even influenced consumers to visit physical stores after seeing products online.

2. Augmented Reality (AR) and Virtual Reality (VR)

AR and VR technologies are being leveraged by social media to provide immersive shopping experiences. Users can try on virtual clothes, visualize furniture in their living spaces, and even "test drive" (practice of trying out or evaluating a product before making a purchase decision) products before buying. This merging of online and offline experiences blurs the lines between traditional and e-commerce shopping.

3. Location-Based Services

Social media platforms often use location-based services to provide users with personalized recommendations and offers. This feature connects online users with local businesses, encouraging them to explore nearby stores and make in-person purchases.

The Dark Side of Social Media on Shopping

While social media has undeniably revolutionized shopping, there are also downsides to consider.

1. Impulse Buying

The constant stream of content on social media can trigger impulse buying. Scrolling through feeds can lead to spur-of-the-moment purchases, which may not always align with consumers' actual needs or preferences.

2. Privacy Concerns

Social media platforms collect vast amounts of user data, which can be used for targeted advertising. While this can make shopping more personalized, it also raises concerns about data privacy and the potential misuse of personal information.

3. Online Shopping Addiction

The ease of shopping on social media can lead to addictive behavior. Some individuals find it challenging to resist the allure of online deals and discounts, leading to excessive and often financially damaging purchases.

The Future of Social Media in Shopping

1. Augmented Reality Shopping

The integration of AR into shopping experiences is likely to become even more sophisticated. Shoppers will be able to virtually try on clothing, test out makeup, or place furniture in their homes with greater realism, enhancing their confidence in online purchases.

2. Enhanced Personalization

Social media platforms will continue to refine their algorithms to provide users with highly personalized shopping recommendations. This will further bridge the gap between consumers' online and offline shopping experiences.

3. AI-Powered Chatbots

AI chatbots will play a significant role in assisting customers with their shopping journeys. These chatbots will provide real-time customer support, answer questions, and guide users through the purchase process.

4. Sustainability and Ethical Shopping

As consumer awareness of environmental and ethical issues grows, social media will likely promote sustainable and ethical shopping choices. Brands that prioritize eco-friendly practices will gain visibility and support on these platforms.

Conclusion

Social media's impact on shopping cannot be overstated. It has transformed the way consumers discover, evaluate, and purchase products. Businesses that understand the dynamics of social media and adapt to its ever-evolving landscape can thrive in this digital age. The influence of social media on shopping trends, consumer behavior, and the convergence of offline and online shopping is undeniable, making it an indispensable tool for businesses and an integral part of consumers' shopping experiences. As the future unfolds, it will be fascinating to witness the continued evolution of social media's role in shaping the world of shopping.

Introduction

In the digital age, shopping has transcended the boundaries of physical stores and leaped into the vast realm of the internet. With the proliferation of e-commerce platforms and online marketplaces, consumers are faced with an overwhelming abundance of choices. In this era of virtual shelves and digital checkouts, the role of customer reviews and ratings has become increasingly significant in shaping consumer decisions. This article delves into the importance of online reviews and ratings in influencing purchasing choices, shedding light on their impact and how they empower consumers.

The World of Shopping: Offline vs. Online

Offline and online shopping represent two distinct worlds, each with its own unique features and characteristics. Offline shopping, the traditional brick-and-mortar experience, offers the opportunity to see, touch, and try products before making a purchase. This setting provides a tangible shopping experience and allows for immediate gratification.

On the other hand, online shopping brings convenience and accessibility to consumers' fingertips. With a vast array of products available at any time, consumers can shop from the comfort of their own homes. However, the absence of physical interaction with products and a sales associate's guidance can make the online shopping experience less intuitive.

The Role of Customer Reviews and Ratings

In both offline and online shopping, customer reviews and ratings play a crucial role in guiding consumer choices. These are essential tools that provide insights into the quality, performance, and overall satisfaction with products or services. However, online platforms have revolutionized the way these reviews and ratings are gathered, shared, and accessed, making them more influential than ever.

1. The Power of Online Reviews

Online reviews, in the form of written feedback, provide detailed accounts of customers' experiences with products or services. They allow shoppers to gain in-depth knowledge about a product's features, durability, and suitability for their needs. Online reviews offer a forum for customers to share their personal anecdotes, both positive and negative, with a wide audience.

For example, when considering the purchase of a new smartphone, a potential buyer can read online reviews to learn about the device's camera quality, battery life, user interface, and any potential drawbacks. These reviews often reveal insights that a product's official description may not include, helping consumers make well-informed decisions.

2. The Influence of Ratings

Ratings, typically represented by stars or numerical values, offer a quick and concise summary of a product's overall satisfaction level. They provide an at-a-glance indication of how a product is generally perceived by those who have purchased it. Higher ratings usually signify a product's quality and reliability.

A product with a high average rating can instill confidence in a buyer's decision. In contrast, a low rating can raise red flags and prompt further investigation before proceeding with a purchase. Ratings are a valuable tool for consumers who want to make quick decisions or compare multiple products at a glance.

The Significance of Online Reviews and Ratings

1. Building Trust and Credibility

Online reviews and ratings contribute to building trust between consumers and sellers. When customers see positive reviews and high ratings, they are more likely to have confidence in the quality of a product or service. Reviews often provide social proof, assuring potential buyers that others have had positive experiences with the product.

This trust is particularly crucial in the online shopping environment, where shoppers cannot physically assess the product. Reviews and ratings act as a surrogate for the salesperson's recommendation, which is prevalent in offline stores. When customers trust other consumers' opinions, they are more likely to make a purchase.

2. Informed Decision-Making

The wealth of information found in online reviews empowers consumers to make well-informed decisions. Shoppers can tap into the collective wisdom of those who have previously purchased the product and learn from their experiences. They can explore different perspectives, including pros and cons, to assess whether a product aligns with their unique preferences and requirements.

Moreover, online reviews often highlight nuances and specific use cases that may not be evident from the product description alone. For example, a laptop that boasts exceptional performance might have overheating issues, a detail that can be crucial for a buyer who plans to use it for resource-intensive tasks.

3. Product Improvement

For sellers and manufacturers, online reviews provide invaluable insights into their products. Customer feedback helps them identify areas for improvement and innovation. When they pay attention to reviews, companies can address customer concerns, fix product flaws, and enhance overall satisfaction.

Moreover, engaged sellers can use online reviews as a direct channel for customer support. They can respond to customer inquiries, resolve issues, and maintain a positive brand image, which further reinforces trust and loyalty among consumers.

4. Community and Social Interaction

Online reviews and ratings also foster a sense of community among consumers. Buyers often read and write reviews to connect with others who share their interests or needs. They can seek advice from like-minded individuals, contributing to a sense of belonging within the online shopping ecosystem.

Moreover, sharing reviews and ratings is a way for consumers to participate in the marketplace and influence its dynamics. In this sense, customers become active participants in the shopping experience, shaping the reputation of products and services.

The Influence on Offline Shopping

While online reviews and ratings are deeply ingrained in the world of e-commerce, their influence is not confined to the virtual realm. These digital tools have spilled over into the offline shopping landscape, altering the dynamics of brick-and-mortar retail.

1. Showrooming and Webrooming

The phenomenon of showrooming and webrooming highlights the interplay between offline and online shopping. Showrooming involves visiting a physical store to evaluate a product in person but ultimately making the purchase online, often due to the availability of better deals or favorable online reviews. Conversely, webrooming refers to researching products online and then making the purchase in a physical store to see and touch the product before buying.

These behaviors illustrate how online reviews and ratings are instrumental in guiding purchasing decisions even in traditional retail settings. Consumers have access to a wealth of information through their smartphones, allowing them to make more informed decisions while in a physical store.

2. Social Validation in Offline Shopping

In offline stores, reviews and ratings also play a role in social validation. When consumers are uncertain about a product, they may use their smartphones to check online reviews and ratings, seeking reassurance from the wider online community.

This practice demonstrates the seamless integration of online and offline shopping experiences. Offline retailers are increasingly recognizing the importance of offering a digital dimension to their stores, such as providing access to online reviews, to cater to the needs of tech-savvy consumers.

Conclusion

The influence of customer reviews and ratings in the world of shopping, both offline and online, is undeniable. These digital tools have become a cornerstone of consumer decision-making, offering a wealth of information, trust-building, and community engagement. Whether shopping in a brick-and-mortar store or navigating the vast landscape of e-commerce, the wisdom of the crowd has become an indispensable companion in the modern shopping journey.

As we continue to navigate the world of offline and online shopping, the power of customer reviews and ratings will only grow. Consumers will rely on these tools to make informed decisions, while sellers and manufacturers will leverage them to improve products, foster trust, and build lasting relationships with their customers. In this interconnected world of commerce, reviews and ratings are here to stay, shaping the future of shopping.

Chapter 13. Price Comparison and Bargain Hunting

Introduction

In today's consumer-driven world, saving money has become a universal pursuit. Whether you're a seasoned shopper or a novice in the world of retail therapy, the thrill of finding a good deal is an experience cherished by all. Price comparison and bargain hunting are two essential skills that can help you achieve substantial savings when making purchases, be it offline or online. This article will delve into the art of finding the best deals, offering strategies and insights to help readers maximize their shopping budget while enjoying the thrill of hunting for bargains.

The Rise of Online Shopping

Online shopping has undergone a meteoric rise in popularity, particularly in the last decade. It offers unparalleled convenience, a vast array of choices, and the ability to shop from the comfort of your own home. However, this convenience comes with the risk of overpaying if you're not vigilant in your quest for the best prices.

Utilizing Online Price Comparison Tools

Online price comparison tools are your best friends when it comes to finding the most competitive prices on the internet. These tools, such as PriceGrabber, Shopzilla, and Google Shopping, allow you to compare prices across multiple retailers, helping you identify the best deals within seconds.

To use these tools effectively:

Start with a Specific Product Search: Input the name or description of the product you want, and the tool will generate a list of prices from various retailers.

Sort and Filter: These tools often provide filters to help you narrow down your options. Sort the results by price, location, or seller ratings to find the most suitable deal.

Check Reviews and Ratings: Don't solely rely on the price. Make sure to read reviews and check seller ratings to ensure a reputable and reliable transaction.

Embracing the Power of Online Coupons

Online coupons and discount codes are a potent weapon in the online shopper's arsenal. Many e-commerce sites and retailers offer promotional codes that can unlock significant discounts. These codes can be found through various means.

Official Websites: Retailers often post coupons and discount codes on their websites. Look for dedicated sections or subscribe to their newsletters for exclusive deals.

Coupon Websites: Websites like RetailMeNot, Coupons.com, and Honey aggregate coupon codes for various online retailers. A simple search can reveal potential savings.

Browser Extensions: Install browser extensions like Honey or Rakuten that automatically search for and apply applicable coupon codes at checkout.

Cashback Offers: Some websites and credit cards offer cashback for online purchases. Be sure to explore these options to save even more.

Offline Shopping: The Thrill of the Hunt

While online shopping offers unbeatable convenience, offline shopping provides a sensory experience that many still treasure. Visiting physical stores, bargaining with sellers, and exploring the shelves can be a fun and rewarding endeavor. However, it's essential to employ a different set of strategies for saving money when shopping offline.

Exploring Local Markets and Flea Markets

Local markets and flea markets can be treasure troves for bargain hunters. These places often feature unique items, handcrafted products, and antiques at a fraction of the cost you'd find in high-end stores. To make the most of your visit:

Go Early: Arriving early at these markets can help you secure the best deals, as sellers are often more willing to negotiate at the start of the day.

Hone Your Bargaining Skills: Negotiation is a key skill in these settings. Be polite, friendly, and willing to haggle. Start with a lower price and work your way up if necessary.

Inspect Thoroughly: Since items at markets may not come with warranties, examine products carefully to ensure they're in good condition before purchasing.

Outlet Malls: Hidden Gems of Offline Shopping

Outlet malls are a haven for savvy shoppers seeking discounts on well-known brands. These shopping centers offer items at significantly reduced prices, often due to overstock, last season's collections, or minor imperfections. To make the most of your outlet mall visit:

Plan Your Trip: Research the brands and deals available at the outlet mall you plan to visit. Make a list of your desired purchases to stay focused.

Timing Matters: Outlets may have clearance sales or special promotions during holidays or end-of-season periods. Timing your visit can lead to substantial savings.

Check for Imperfections: While most outlet items are brand-new, it's essential to inspect for any imperfections that may have caused the discount.

Join Loyalty Programs: Many outlet stores offer loyalty programs that provide additional discounts and exclusive offers. Sign up and take advantage of these perks.

The Best of Both Worlds: Hybrid Shopping

Hybrid shopping, a combination of online and offline shopping, allows you to capitalize on the strengths of both worlds and maximize your savings. Here's how to navigate this approach:

Research Online, Buy Offline: Use online resources to research products and find the best deals. Once you've identified the right item and a good price, visit a local store to make the purchase.

In-Store Price Matching: Some brick-and-mortar retailers offer price matching, allowing you to enjoy the convenience of shopping in person while benefiting from online prices.

Curbside Pickup: Curbside pickup is a retail service that allows customers to order products online or by phone and then collect their purchases at a designated area near the store's entrance or at the curb, often without leaving their vehicle. This service offers convenience and minimizes in-store contact. Many stores now offer curbside pickup for online orders. This lets you enjoy the online shopping experience while avoiding shipping costs and receiving immediate access to your purchases.

Returns and Exchanges: Consider the ease of returning or exchanging items when choosing where to shop. Physical stores often provide more convenient options for returns and exchanges.

Price Comparison Apps: Your Shopping Sidekick

Price comparison apps have become indispensable tools for modern shoppers. These mobile apps provide real-time price comparisons, reviews, and product information to help you make informed decisions while on the go. Some of the top price comparison apps include:

ShopSavvy: Scan barcodes to find the best prices for products and read user reviews.

Price.com: Discover deals and discounts across various categories, including electronics, fashion, and more.

Shopzilla: Access price comparisons, product reviews, and deals from various retailers.

Shopkick: Earn rewards and discounts while you shop both online and offline.

BuyVia: Find local deals and compare prices online, ensuring you're getting the best possible price.

Staying Cautious: Avoiding Pitfalls

While price comparison and bargain hunting are essential skills, it's equally crucial to stay cautious to avoid common pitfalls.

Beware of Scams: Be wary of deals that seem too good to be true, especially from unknown or suspicious websites. Research the seller's credibility and read reviews before making a purchase.

Shipping Costs: Don't forget to account for shipping costs when comparing online prices. Sometimes, a seemingly cheaper online deal can become more expensive once shipping fees are included.

Return Policies: Always review the return policies of online retailers. In some cases, return shipping costs can eat into your savings.

Security: Ensure that your online shopping experience is secure by using trusted websites and keeping your payment information safe. Look for the padlock symbol in the address bar to indicate a secure connection.

Conclusion: The Art of Price Comparison and Bargain Hunting

In the dynamic world of shopping, mastering the art of price comparison and bargain hunting can make a substantial difference in your finances. Whether you prefer the convenience of online shopping or the thrill of visiting physical stores, these strategies can help you find the best deals and make the most of your budget. Stay vigilant, explore new avenues, and embrace technology to navigate the ever-evolving landscape of shopping while maximizing your savings. After all, in the world of consumerism, a well-hunted bargain is a treasure worth celebrating.

Introduction

In the ever-evolving landscape of retail, the concept of returns and customer service plays a pivotal role in shaping consumers' perceptions and experiences. Both offline and online shopping channels offer unique avenues for consumers to explore, but their processes for returning items and the quality of customer support significantly differ. This article delves into the world of returns and customer service, shedding light on the processes involved and comparing the quality of service in both offline and online retail environments.

The Return Process in Offline Retail

The return process in offline retail has been a long-standing tradition. Customers have been walking into brick-and-mortar stores for decades to return products. This experience is characterized by several key elements.

In-Person Interaction: In offline retail, customers visit the physical store where the purchase was made to return items. This personal interaction allows for immediate problem-solving and real-time communication with store employees.

Tangible Returns: Offline returns usually involve physically bringing the item to the store, along with the original receipt. The returned product is inspected on-site, and refunds or exchanges are processed in real-time.

Human Element: The in-store experience benefits from the human element, as employees can provide immediate assistance, answer questions, and guide customers through the return process.

Immediate Resolution: In most cases, returns are processed instantly, providing customers with a quick resolution to their concerns.

The Return Process in Online Retail

Online shopping has gained immense popularity, offering convenience and a wide range of products. However, the return process in online retail comes with its own unique characteristics.

Digital Communication: Online retailers have to rely on digital channels for return requests and communication. Customers often initiate the process through emails or the retailer's website.

Shipping and Handling: Returning an item online typically involves repackaging the product and sending it back through a shipping service. This can lead to additional costs for customers, and the shipping process can take time.

Digital Documentation: Online retailers may require customers to fill out return forms and provide digital documentation. This may include photos of the product or proof of purchase.

Processing Time: The return process in online retail can be slower than its offline counterpart, as it depends on the time it takes for the product to be shipped back, inspected, and a refund or replacement to be processed.

Quality of Customer Service in Offline Retail

In offline retail, the quality of customer service is often a defining factor that sets apart one store from another. The following factors contribute to the quality of customer service in offline retail:

Face-to-Face Interaction: The in-person nature of offline retail enables direct and immediate communication between customers and store employees. This face-to-face interaction can lead to better understanding and quicker issue resolution.

Personalization: Offline retail excels in personalization, as employees can build relationships with customers. Online retail, while attempting personalization through data analysis, can sometimes come off as impersonal.

Expertise: In physical stores, employees are well-trained and can provide expert assistance. Online retail relies on product descriptions and customer reviews, which may lack the depth of expertise.

Transparency: Both offline and online retailers need to maintain transparent policies regarding returns, warranties, and other customer-related matters. This helps build trust and ensures a smooth return process.

Customer Reviews: Customer reviews and feedback play a significant role in online retail. Retailers who respond to customer reviews, both positive and negative, can showcase their commitment to customer service.

Quality of Customer Service in Online Retail

Online retailers face a unique set of challenges and opportunities in providing customer service. The quality of customer service in online retail is shaped by the following elements:

Digital Communication: Online retailers rely on digital channels for customer communication. This can sometimes result in delayed responses, and miscommunication can occur due to the lack of face-to-face interaction.

User-Friendly Websites: A well-designed website with a user-friendly interface is crucial for providing quality customer service. Customers should be able to easily find information, contact support, and initiate returns.

Responsive Customer Support: Providing timely responses to customer inquiries, including return requests and concerns, is essential for good customer service in online retail.

Transparency: Both offline and online retailers should clearly communicate return policies, warranties, and terms and conditions. In the case of online retailers, providing step-by-step guides for the return process can be beneficial.

Customer Feedback: Encouraging customer feedback and addressing concerns promptly, whether through in-person interactions or online communication. Using feedback to make improvements in the shopping experience and return process.

Comparing Offline and Online Retail Customer Service

Let's compare the quality of customer service in both offline and online retail environments.

Convenience: Offline retail offers immediate convenience through face-to-face interactions and quick returns, but it might not be suitable for customers who live far from physical stores. Online retail offers convenience in terms of access but may have delayed resolution times for returns.

Personalization: Offline retail excels in personalization, as employees can build relationships with customers. Online retail, while attempting personalization through data analysis, can sometimes come off as impersonal.

Expertise: In offline retail, employees are well-trained and can provide expert assistance. Online retail relies on product descriptions and customer reviews, which may lack the depth of expertise.

Transparency: Both offline and online retailers need to maintain transparent policies, but online retailers need to be especially clear, as customers may not physically see the products.

Customer Feedback: Online retail relies heavily on customer feedback and reviews, which can be a double-edged sword. While feedback can inform potential buyers, negative reviews can damage a brand's reputation.

Improving Returns and Customer Service in Both Channels

Enhancing the return process and customer service in both offline and online retail is crucial for maintaining and growing a customer base. Here are some strategies to improve customer service:

In-Person Customer Service in Offline Retail:

> ➤ Ongoing training for staff to improve expertise and problem-solving skills.
> ➤ Implementing technology, such as in-store kiosks, to streamline the return process and gather customer feedback.
> ➤ *In-store kiosks* are self-service terminals or machines located within physical retail stores, allowing customers to perform various tasks independently. These tasks may include browsing and ordering products, checking product availability, making payments, printing tickets, and accessing information, enhancing the shopping experience and providing convenience.

Online Customer Service in Online Retail:

> ➤ Establishing a dedicated customer service team to provide quick and helpful responses.
> ➤ Enhancing user-friendly websites and mobile apps for seamless navigation and communication.

Personalization in Both Channels:

> ➤ Offline retailers can introduce loyalty programs and customized offers to improve personalization.
> ➤ Online retailers can use data analytics to recommend products and personalize the online shopping experience.

Transparent Policies in Both Channels:

> ➢ Both offline and online retailers should clearly communicate return policies, warranties, and terms and conditions.
> ➢ In the case of online retailers, providing step-by-step guides for the return process can be beneficial.

Customer Feedback:

> ➢ Encouraging customer feedback and addressing concerns promptly, whether through in-person interactions or online communication.
> ➢ Using feedback to make improvements in the shopping experience and return process.

Conclusion

Returns and customer service play an essential role in shaping the retail landscape, whether it's through offline or online channels. The choice between the two often boils down to convenience, personalization, and the quality of service. While offline retail offers face-to-face interactions and immediate resolutions, online retail provides access to a vast array of products and services.

Both offline and online retailers can learn from each other's strengths and weaknesses to improve customer service. The key lies in understanding the unique attributes of each channel and tailoring their approach to meet the evolving expectations of today's consumers. Ultimately, the goal is to provide a seamless and satisfying shopping experience that keeps customers coming back for more.

Introduction

Online shopping has revolutionized the way we buy products and services. It offers convenience, a wide variety of choices, and the ability to shop from the comfort of our homes. However, with this convenience comes the risk of online shopping fraud. As technology advances, so do the tactics of cybercriminals who aim to exploit the vulnerabilities of e-commerce platforms and unsuspecting consumers. In this article, we will explore common online shopping frauds and provide guidance on how to protect yourself from scams and fraudulent transactions. Navigating the world of online shopping requires vigilance, awareness, and a proactive approach to fraud prevention.

Types of Online Shopping Frauds

1. Phishing Scams

Phishing scams involve cybercriminals impersonating legitimate businesses or organizations to deceive consumers into revealing sensitive information, such as credit card details or login credentials. These scams typically occur through fake emails, websites, or text messages. It's crucial to recognize the red flags of phishing attempts, including spelling errors, unsolicited communication, and suspicious links.

2. Fake Online Stores

Fake online stores are websites that mimic well-known e-commerce platforms, offering counterfeit products or non-existent items. Consumers are enticed by enticing deals and discounts, only to receive subpar or counterfeit products, or never receive their orders at all. It's essential to verify the legitimacy of an online store by checking reviews, researching the company, and using secure payment methods.

3. Auction Fraud

Online auction platforms can be a breeding ground for fraud, with scammers using various tactics to manipulate auctions, misrepresent products, or disappear after receiving payment. Buyers and sellers should exercise caution, communicate transparently, and use reputable auction sites with established dispute resolution processes.

4. Credit Card Fraud

Credit card fraud involves the unauthorized use of someone's credit card information to make online purchases. Fraudsters may obtain this information through data breaches, card skimming, or phishing. Protect yourself by regularly monitoring your credit card statements, using strong and unique passwords, and enabling two-factor authentication where available.

5. Shipping and Delivery Scams

In shipping and delivery scams, fraudsters often pose as courier companies or package delivery services, claiming there is an issue with your order and requesting personal or payment information. Always verify the authenticity of such messages directly with the retailer or courier company and avoid sharing sensitive data via unsolicited requests.

Prevention and Protection Measures

1. Secure Your Devices

A crucial first step in online shopping fraud prevention is to secure your devices. Ensure your computer, smartphone, and tablet have up-to-date antivirus software, firewalls, and operating systems. Regularly update your browsers to protect against known vulnerabilities that scammers may exploit.

2. Use Trusted Websites

Stick to well-established and reputable e-commerce websites. If you're uncertain about a specific site, do some research before making a purchase. Check for online reviews and look for signs of trustworthiness, such as SSL certificates, a privacy policy, and a physical address for the company.

3. Avoid Public Wi-Fi

Public Wi-Fi networks are often less secure and can be a breeding ground for cybercriminals. Avoid making online purchases while connected to public Wi-Fi, as it increases the risk of your personal and financial information being intercepted.

4. Strong Passwords and Two-Factor Authentication

Create strong and unique passwords for your online shopping accounts. Use a combination of letters, numbers, and symbols, and avoid using easily guessable information like your name or birthdate. Additionally, enable two-factor authentication whenever it's available. This provides an extra layer of security by requiring you to enter a code sent to your mobile device to access your account.

5. Be Wary of Emails and Messages

Phishing attacks often begin with a deceptive email or message. Be cautious when receiving unsolicited communications that ask for personal or financial information. Verify the sender's authenticity, look for spelling and grammar errors, and avoid clicking on suspicious links.

6. Check for Secure Connections

Before entering payment information on a website, ensure that the connection is secure. Look for "https://" in the URL and a padlock symbol in the address bar. These indicators signify that the website encrypts your data during transmission.

7. Monitor Your Accounts

Regularly monitor your bank and credit card statements for unauthorized transactions. If you notice any suspicious activity, contact your financial institution immediately. Early detection can help prevent further fraudulent charges.

8. Trust Your Instincts

If a deal seems too good to be true, it probably is. Be cautious of heavily discounted products, especially on lesser-known websites. Scammers often lure victims with unrealistically low prices to trick them into making a quick purchase.

9. Read Reviews and Do Research

Before making a purchase, read product reviews and check the reputation of the seller. Pay attention to both positive and negative feedback, and be skeptical of products with few or no reviews.

10. Use Secure Payment Methods

When making online purchases, use secure payment methods such as credit cards or digital wallets that offer fraud protection and dispute resolution. Avoid using methods that offer little recourse, such as wire transfers or prepaid gift cards.

Typically, credit cards are considered more secure than wire transfers when it comes to online transactions. Credit cards often offer fraud protection and dispute resolution services to their users. If unauthorized or fraudulent charges occur, users can usually report them to the credit card company, and the charges can be investigated and potentially reversed. This provides an additional layer of security and recourse for consumers.

In contrast, wire transfers, once executed, are generally difficult to reverse, and they offer fewer protections against fraud or unauthorized transactions. Therefore, if there's a dispute or fraudulent activity involving a wire transfer, it can be more challenging to resolve compared to using a credit card.

It's essential to note that security may also depend on the specific policies and protections offered by your financial institution and the terms of the service you are using.

11. Keep Records

Keep records of your online transactions, including order confirmation emails, receipts, and tracking information. These documents may be essential if you encounter any issues with your order.

12. Report Suspected Fraud

If you suspect that you have fallen victim to online shopping fraud, report it to the relevant authorities, such as your local law enforcement and the Federal Trade Commission (FTC) in the United States. Timely reporting can help prevent further scams and protect other potential victims.

Conclusion

Online shopping offers unparalleled convenience and accessibility to a vast array of products and services, but it also comes with inherent risks of fraud and scams. By staying informed, practicing vigilance, and following the preventive measures outlined in this article, you can protect yourself from online shopping fraud. In the ever-evolving world of e-commerce, the key to safe and enjoyable online shopping experiences is to shop smart, stay aware, and prioritize security. Remember that while fraud prevention measures are essential, they should not deter you from enjoying the many benefits of online shopping.

Introduction

Shopping, an activity deeply embedded in our modern lifestyle, holds more power than we often realize. With the advent of both offline and online shopping, consumers have more options at their fingertips than ever before. However, with great power comes great responsibility. This article delves into the importance of ethical and sustainable shopping and aims to encourage responsible consumer behavior. As we navigate the world of shopping, understanding and practicing sustainability and ethical considerations is imperative for a brighter future.

The Urgency of Ethical and Sustainable Shopping

Before we explore the nuances of ethical and sustainable shopping, it is vital to understand the urgency of these considerations in today's consumer landscape.

1. Environmental Impact

The environmental cost of our consumer choices cannot be ignored. From greenhouse gas emissions associated with manufacturing and transportation to the excessive waste generated by disposable products, our shopping habits contribute significantly to climate change and environmental degradation.

2. Labor Exploitation

The fashion industry, among others, has come under scrutiny for unethical labor practices. Sweatshops, child labor, and subpar working conditions are all too common in the race for lower production costs. A *sweatshop* is a workplace, typically in the manufacturing sector, where employees, often under poor conditions, work long hours for low wages, and may be subject to exploitation and unsafe working conditions. Sweatshops have been widely criticized for their treatment of workers and have been the subject of efforts to improve labor rights and working conditions. As consumers, we play a role in supporting or opposing such practices.

3. Social Responsibility

Our purchasing decisions can either support or undermine socially responsible businesses. By choosing to buy from companies that give back to their communities or actively promote social equity, we can be a part of positive change.

Ethical Shopping: Making Choices with Values

1. Transparent Supply Chains

One of the cornerstones of ethical shopping is a transparent supply chain. When consumers have access to information about the sourcing and production of the products they buy, they can make informed choices. Companies that provide this transparency often have nothing to hide and are more likely to follow ethical practices.

2. Fair Trade Products

Fair trade products are goods, typically agricultural or handcrafted items, that are produced and traded under specific social and environmental standards aimed at ensuring fair compensation for producers, ethical working conditions, and sustainability. The goal of fair trade is to empower farmers and artisans in developing countries, promote social and economic equity, and support environmentally responsible practices. These products are often labeled as "Fair Trade Certified".

Purchasing products with the Fair Trade certification is an excellent way to support ethical practices. These products are often produced by workers who receive fair wages and operate in safe conditions. The Fair Trade label ensures that the product meets specific social and environmental standards.

3. Supporting Local Businesses

Local businesses often have a more direct and transparent connection to their communities. By choosing to shop locally, you can support businesses that contribute to your area's economic development and engage in responsible practices.

4. Conscious Consumption

The concept of conscious consumption encourages buyers to consider the lifespan of the products they purchase. Opting for quality over quantity, repairing items instead of discarding them, and buying second-hand are all strategies to reduce waste and support ethical consumerism.

Sustainable Shopping: Minimizing Environmental Impact

1. Eco-Friendly Products

Many companies are now prioritizing eco-friendly products. These are designed with sustainability in mind, utilizing materials and production methods that reduce the environmental impact. Look for products that are made from renewable resources, are biodegradable, or can be easily recycled.

2. Energy-Efficient Choices

Consider the energy efficiency of the products you purchase. Appliances, electronics, and vehicles all have varying levels of energy efficiency. Opting for products that consume less energy can significantly reduce your carbon footprint.

3. Reducing Plastic Usage

Plastic pollution is a pressing global issue. Be conscious of your plastic usage by choosing products with minimal plastic packaging, carrying reusable bags, and opting for products made from alternative materials.

4. Minimizing Food Waste

Food waste is a substantial environmental problem. Shop with a plan, avoid overbuying, and make use of leftovers. Composting is an excellent way to reduce food waste's impact on landfills. *Composting* is the natural process of decomposing organic materials, like kitchen scraps, into nutrient-rich soil conditioner, known as compost, that can enrich garden soil and reduce waste.

Technology's Role in Ethical and Sustainable Shopping

1. Online Shopping Platforms

The rise of e-commerce has transformed the way we shop. Online platforms like Amazon, eBay, and many others offer convenience and a vast array of products. However, ethical and sustainable considerations should still apply. Research and choose sellers that align with your values.

2. Apps and Websites

Numerous apps and websites help consumers make ethical and sustainable choices. These platforms provide information about a product's origins, its ethical or sustainable certifications, and even user reviews regarding the company's practices.

3. Price Comparison Tools

Price comparison tools can help you find the best deals, which can be a part of ethical and sustainable shopping. Reducing expenses can lead to less wasteful consumption and a smaller environmental footprint.

4. Delivery and Shipping

While the convenience of home delivery is undeniable, it often involves carbon emissions from transportation. Consider consolidation of orders to reduce the number of shipments or explore options like carbon-neutral delivery services (transportation and delivery methods that offset their carbon emissions by investing in environmental initiatives, such as reforestation or renewable energy projects, to achieve a net-zero carbon footprint).

The Role of Certification and Labeling

1. Eco-Certifications

Eco-certifications are official endorsements or labels granted to products, services, or organizations that meet specific environmental standards, indicating their commitment to sustainability and responsible practices. Look for eco-certifications on products, such as the Energy Star label for energy-efficient electronics or the USDA Organic label for food products. These certifications indicate adherence to specific environmental standards.

2. Ethical Certifications

Ethical certifications are official designations or labels given to products, services, or organizations that adhere to established ethical standards and practices, demonstrating their commitment to principles such as fair labor, social responsibility, and ethical sourcing. Various ethical certifications, such as Fair Trade and B Corp, demonstrate a company's commitment to social and environmental responsibility. Supporting products with these certifications can be a vote for ethical business practices.

3. The Power of Consumer Demand

As consumers demand more transparency and ethical practices from businesses, companies are increasingly adopting certifications and labeling to meet this demand. The power lies with consumers to drive positive change through their purchasing choices.

Challenges and Obstacles

1. Price Considerations

One of the significant challenges in ethical and sustainable shopping is the perception that it is more expensive. While some products may indeed have higher price points due to responsible practices, this is not universally true. In the long run, the durability and quality of sustainable products can offset the initial cost.

2. Lack of Information

Not all companies provide detailed information about their supply chains or ethical practices. Consumers may face difficulties making informed choices without access to this information.

3. Greenwashing

Greenwashing is the deceptive practice of portraying a company or product as environmentally friendly when it is not. Detecting greenwashing can be challenging, but vigilant consumers can rely on third-party certifications and independent reviews to make more informed decisions.

Personal Responsibility and Collective Impact

1. Leading by Example

Individual consumers have the power to lead by example, influencing friends and family to adopt ethical and sustainable shopping practices. Your choices can inspire others to consider their consumer habits.

2. Advocacy and Activism

Beyond individual action, collective efforts can drive change. Advocacy for ethical and sustainable practices, supporting organizations that work toward these goals, and participating in relevant campaigns can all make a difference.

3. Business Responsibility

While consumers bear the responsibility of making ethical and sustainable choices, businesses also play a pivotal role. It is crucial for companies to adopt these practices voluntarily and transparently. Government regulations and incentives can also promote corporate responsibility.

Conclusion

Ethical and sustainable shopping is more than just a trend; it is a necessity for our planet's health and the well-being of future generations. As we navigate the world of offline and online shopping, the choices we make can either exacerbate environmental issues, support unethical practices, or contribute to positive change.

Consumers have the power to influence the marketplace by voting with their wallets, supporting companies that prioritize sustainability and ethics. As technology continues to shape the way we shop, it is essential to leverage online resources and tools to make informed choices.

In conclusion, the importance of ethical and sustainable shopping cannot be overstated. Our responsibility as consumers is not limited to buying products; it extends to making conscious, informed decisions that align with our values. Through ethical and sustainable shopping, we can create a world where businesses prioritize the planet, people, and ethical practices. The power to make a difference is in our hands, and it begins with the choices we make every day.

Introduction

Shopping, an age-old activity that has long been a cornerstone of human life, has been undergoing a profound transformation in recent years. The convergence of online and offline retail experiences has created a dynamic and ever-evolving landscape that presents both challenges and opportunities. In this article, we will explore the future of shopping, taking into account emerging technologies, shifting consumer expectations, and the likely evolution of the retail sector.

The Digital Revolution: Augmented Reality and Virtual Reality

One of the most significant shifts in the future of shopping is the growing prominence of augmented reality (AR) and virtual reality (VR). These technologies have the potential to reshape the way consumers interact with products before making a purchase. Retailers are increasingly incorporating AR and VR into their shopping experiences, allowing customers to virtually try on clothes, visualize furniture in their homes, or test out products before buying.

AR, for example, enables consumers to see how a piece of furniture would fit into their living space by superimposing a virtual image of the item over their camera feed. This technology not only enhances the shopping experience but also reduces the risk of post-purchase disappointment. As these technologies become more accessible and refined, they are likely to become integral components of the shopping journey.

Personalization: The Key to Customer Satisfaction

As e-commerce platforms and physical retailers become increasingly interconnected, personalization will play a central role in the future of shopping. Retailers are leveraging data analytics and artificial intelligence (AI) to create highly personalized shopping experiences. This means that consumers will see product recommendations, deals, and advertisements tailored to their preferences and past behavior.

Imagine walking into a store, and the displays automatically adjust to your style and preferences based on your previous online shopping history. Moreover, online stores could use real-time data to suggest items based on your current mood or interests. Such personalization is not only convenient for shoppers but also beneficial for retailers, as it enhances customer engagement and loyalty.

The Rise of Omnichannel Shopping

The future of shopping is undeniably omnichannel. Consumers are increasingly blurring the lines between online and offline shopping, and retailers are adapting to this shift. The concept of "click and collect" is becoming more prevalent, where customers can order products online and pick them up in-store, enjoying the best of both worlds.

Moreover, physical stores are becoming showrooms and experience centers rather than just transactional spaces. Retailers are harnessing technology to integrate the offline and online experience seamlessly. This shift towards an omnichannel approach enables retailers to meet consumers where they are, fostering convenience and enhancing the shopping journey.

Sustainability and Ethical Shopping

The future of shopping will be marked by a heightened awareness of environmental and ethical concerns. Consumers are increasingly conscious of the impact their purchases have on the planet and the well-being of workers along the supply chain. Retailers are responding by making sustainability a central part of their business strategies.

Eco-friendly packaging, ethical sourcing, and carbon-neutral supply chains are becoming industry standards. Consumers will have access to more information about the products they buy, enabling them to make more informed choices based on their values. In this evolving landscape, retailers who embrace sustainability will likely gain a competitive advantage.

Artificial Intelligence and Chatbots

AI-driven chatbots are becoming an essential part of the shopping experience. They provide customers with instant assistance and information, making the process of finding and purchasing products more efficient. These chatbots can answer questions, recommend products, and guide customers through the shopping journey.

As AI technology continues to advance, these chatbots will become more sophisticated, offering highly personalized interactions that mimic human conversations. This will not only enhance the customer experience but also free up human staff to focus on more complex tasks.

Blockchain and Supply Chain Transparency

Blockchain technology is being increasingly integrated into the retail sector, particularly in ensuring supply chain transparency. It allows consumers to trace the journey of a product from its origin to the store shelf, providing assurance about the authenticity and quality of the item.

Blockchain technology can also play a pivotal role in reducing counterfeit goods, which is a significant concern in the retail industry. With blockchain, consumers can verify the authenticity of luxury products, pharmaceuticals, and other high-value items, enhancing trust in the brands and retailers.

3D Printing and Customization

The future of shopping may witness a surge in 3D printing and customization options. This technology allows consumers to design and create their own products or tailor existing ones to their preferences. From personalized clothing to custom-made furniture, 3D printing offers limitless possibilities.

Customers can choose the color, shape, and features of a product, and it can be manufactured on-demand, reducing waste and overproduction. Retailers that embrace 3D printing and customization will cater to a growing demand for unique and tailor-made products.

Contactless and Frictionless Payments

Contactless payments, already on the rise, will continue to gain ground. Mobile wallets, QR code payments, and other cashless options are becoming more prevalent in physical stores. In addition to being convenient, contactless payments can help reduce physical contact and enhance overall hygiene.

Moreover, as biometric authentication technology improves, consumers may soon be able to complete transactions using facial recognition or fingerprint scans, further streamlining the payment process. The future of shopping will prioritize fast and secure payment methods that minimize friction.

The Role of Data and Privacy Concerns

As shopping becomes increasingly digitized, the collection and use of consumer data will be a crucial aspect of the retail landscape. While personalization relies on data, it also raises important privacy concerns. The future will likely see a delicate balancing act between delivering tailored shopping experiences and respecting consumer privacy.

Regulations like the European Union's General Data Protection Regulation (GDPR) and the California Consumer Privacy Act (CCPA) have already started to shape data practices in the retail sector. As more regions adopt similar regulations, retailers will need to navigate the intricacies of data management to maintain consumer trust.

The Future of Physical Retail

Physical stores are not disappearing; instead, they are evolving. While e-commerce has certainly disrupted the traditional retail model, there will always be a place for brick-and-mortar stores. However, the role of physical stores will shift from being primarily transactional to becoming experiential.

Retailers will need to create unique in-store experiences that cannot be replicated online. These experiences may include interactive product demonstrations, workshops, and events that draw customers into the physical space. Moreover, physical stores can serve as convenient pick-up points for online orders and provide opportunities for consumers to see and touch products before making a purchase.

Last-Mile Delivery and Autonomous Vehicles

The last-mile delivery problem, which involves efficiently delivering products from distribution centers to customers' doorsteps, remains a challenge for online retailers. In the future, autonomous vehicles and drones are expected to play a pivotal role in addressing this issue.

Autonomous delivery vehicles and drones offer the potential for faster, more cost-effective, and environmentally friendly delivery solutions. Companies like Amazon and Google are already testing these technologies, and as they become more reliable and widely adopted, they will transform the way products are delivered to consumers.

Voice Commerce and Smart Assistants

Voice commerce is another emerging trend in the future of shopping. Virtual voice assistants like Amazon's Alexa and Google Assistant are becoming integral parts of the shopping experience. Consumers can place orders, get product recommendations, and check prices through voice commands.

The convenience of voice commerce is likely to drive its adoption further, especially for routine purchases. Retailers that optimize their online stores for voice search and integrate with virtual assistants will have an advantage in this space.

Conclusion

The future of shopping is a fascinating journey into the convergence of online and offline retail. Emerging technologies, shifting consumer expectations, and the evolving retail landscape are reshaping the way we buy and interact with products. From augmented reality and personalization to sustainability and blockchain, the retail sector is in a constant state of transformation.

In this ever-changing environment, successful retailers will be those that embrace innovation, adapt to consumer preferences, and strike the right balance between data utilization and privacy. The key to navigating the world of shopping in the future is to stay agile, anticipate trends, and create seamless, customer-centric shopping experiences that provide both convenience and enjoyment. As we move forward, it's clear that the future of shopping will be marked by exciting possibilities, and the retail landscape will continue to evolve to meet the needs and desires of modern consumers.

In "Navigating the World of Offline and Online Shopping", we embark on a comprehensive journey through the ever-evolving realm of consumerism. This book is your ultimate guide to understanding the intricacies of shopping, both in physical stores and the digital marketplace. From the historical roots of shopping to the latest online trends, we delve into the psychology of consumer behavior and explore the innovations shaping offline and online retail experiences.

With a focus on bridging the gap between traditional and digital shopping, this book addresses crucial aspects such as payment methods, security, social media influence, ethical considerations, and more. Whether you're a seasoned shopper or just beginning your consumer journey, this book offers invaluable insights and strategies for making informed, secure, and ethical shopping choices. Join us as we navigate the present and future of shopping, providing you with the knowledge and tools to be a conscious and confident consumer in a dynamic retail landscape.

ABOUT THE AUTHOR

Mr. C. P. Kumar is a retired Scientist 'G' from National Institute of Hydrology, Roorkee, Uttarakhand, India. He is also a Reiki Healer and Chakra Balancing practitioner (with pendulum dowsing) and offers Emotional Freedom Technique (EFT) to help individuals with emotional issues. Mr. Kumar has authored many books on technical, spiritual, and social topics.

For further details, you may visit his webpage
https://www.angelfire.com/nh/cpkumar/virgo.html